CIVIL SERVICE DEPARTMENT

Introducing Computers

by
Murray
Laver

LONDON: HER MAJESTY'S STATIONERY OFFICE: 1973

The cover illustration is a photo-
micrograph by Paul Brierley of a
single ferrite ring known as a
magnetic core, which is actually about
the size of a letter o.
Ten million of these, threaded on
the wires shown in plate 7, form the
memory of one type of large
computer.
Its function is explained on page 27.

SBN 11 630323 9

Contents

Chapter		Page
1	Image and Reality	1
2	Computer Evolution	3
3	Structure and Function	7
4	Input and Output	14
5	Files	20
6	Electronic Arithmetic	24
7	Overall Control	29
8	On Programming	32
9	Sums for Scientists	37
10	Electronics and the Office	40
11	Computers for Process Control	44
12	Computers in Management	46
13	Computers and the Professions	51
14	Electronic Brains	55
15	Living with Computers	58
Appendix	Reading List	60

Illustrations

Plate

1   The computer room Post Office LACES Centre

2   A visual display unit (VDU)

3   A console

4   A line printer

5   Magnetic tape

6   A disk pack (RDU)

7   A core store plane

8   An integrated circuit

9   A logic bay

10   An OCR reader/sorter

11   A light pen

12   A small Argus computer

Fig. 1 The Parts of an A.D.P. System	Page	8
Fig. 2 Ledger Posting by A.D.P.	,,	10
Fig. 3 Flow Chart, Ledger Posting	,,	11
Fig. 4 Machine Fonts	,,	15
Fig. 5 7-track Punched Paper Tape	,,	16
Fig. 6 80-column Punched Card	,,	17
Fig. 7 Binary Adding Circuit	,,	25

1 Image and Reality

To most laymen, a computer is a complicated electronic machine that performs abstruse calculations at unimaginable speeds, and it is not at all obvious how such a machine can be useful in an ordinary office dealing with simple commercial arithmetic. The explanations offered are often cluttered with jargon and sprinkled with spectacular statistics designed to stupefy the novice.

The press, television and radio are of course accustomed to stress the odd or exciting elements in their news in order to bind the attention of their audiences, and it is sensational stories about the use of computers that receive the widest publicity. We read of them playing chess, choosing names for new drugs or challenging St Paul's authorship of the epistles, and the impression is given that electronic brains are ready to take over all our decisions and much of our thinking. In all this the cautious qualifications of the experienced are omitted and those who have struggled with the difficult problems presented by the use of computers can be forgiven a certain cynicism. They, at least, have learned that computers are no substitute for human thought: indeed, that preparing to put work on to a computer is one of the most mind-stretching exercises that anyone is asked to do.

Nevertheless, we must recognise that the cynicism of the expert is a mental battle scar which will no doubt heal, and we should take care not to recoil too far from the extravagances of the 'electronic wonder machine'. As Lady Lovelace wrote more than a century ago of Charles Babbage's invention of the computer—which he called the 'Analytical Engine':

It is desirable to guard against the possibility of exaggerated ideas that might arise as to the powers of the Analytical Engine. In considering any new subject, there is frequently a tendency, first, to overrate what we find to be already interesting or remarkable; and secondly, by a sort of natural reaction, to undervalue the true state of the case when we do discover that our notions have surpassed those that were really tenable. The analytical engine has no pretensions whatever to originate anything. It can do whatever we know how to order it to perform.

Her last sentence provides a key to the whole subject. If we do not ourselves know how to perform a certain calculation or analytical process, then the computer cannot tell us how to do so. We have to tell it. If it had not been so heavily over-sold, it would not be necessary to state what is obvious to common sense, namely that the computer is just a tool, albeit a very powerful machine tool, and that its effectiveness depends essentially

1

on the skill, experience and ability of the men who select, direct and control its use.

The public image of the computer is of an electronic brain epitomising the incomprehensibility of science. The reality is a simple machine, or rather a group of simple machines whose actions are co-ordinated by a central automatic control. Some of these machines are electronic and some mechanical; acting together they are able to perform arithmetic and such simple logical processes as comparing or sorting items, they can take in information to be 'processed', hold it while it is being worked on, and issue results.

It is the comprehensiveness of their automatic control which is the essentially novel feature of computers. Automatic machines are not new but their control arrangements usually achieve only very specific results; for example, a machine designed to count banknotes does this very well but can do nothing else. The control arrangements of computers are not specific: they can be pre-set to carry out any of a virtually unlimited variety of processes. This is achieved by putting into the computer a program* of instructions which sets out in complete detail the required sequence of operations. The program of instructions remains in the computer while it is doing the job for which that program was prepared, and is replaced by another when a different job is to be done.

The simpler kinds of mechanical calculator can be regarded as having built-in programs, which are unchangeable and also severely limited in the number and variety of the successive steps that can be executed. A computer's program can direct it automatically through many hundreds or thousands of steps, and can be replaced by one for a quite different process in a matter of a few minutes. The difference between these two types of machine in some ways resembles the difference between a musical box—able to play a single short melody, and a gramophone—able to play any of a wide and ever-growing variety of records. A computer without a program is like a gramophone without a record. A payroll program makes it temporarily a special-purpose payroll machine. Replacing the payroll program by a statistical program converts it for the time being into a special-purpose statistical machine. Replacing that by a scientific program makes it operate as a scientific calculator, and so on.

The modern computer stands at the end of a long line of mechanical aids to calculation and is distinguished from them not by any magical new method of reasoning or calculation but by being automatic, general-purpose and fast. It is not just the latest scientific toy, but has appeared at this time because techniques have been developed in the last decade or two which provide a means of meeting the pressing demands for more and more calculation which arose first in the applied sciences. Thus, the use of computers is not a passing fashion, but a new and significant advance in the handling of data for science, industry and commerce.

See plates 1 & 12

---

*This is an accepted British spelling.

2 Computer Evolution

THIS chapter gives a brief account of the history of mechanical aids to calculation in order to show that the computer occupies a natural position in an evolutionary series.

History and the widespread use of the decimal number system together show that the first aids to calculation were the fingers; and the word 'digit' derives from the Latin for finger. Quite elaborate systems of finger reckoning were developed and widely used until a few centuries ago.

The first known calculating machine is the abacus—a name which may derive from a Semitic word meaning dust or sand. The most primitive form of abacus consisted of a sand tray in which lines could be drawn by the fingers and on which pebbles were placed to indicate the numbers taking part in the calculation: the Latin for pebbles gives our word 'calculation'. The abacus was used by the Greeks and Romans in pre-Christian times and was known to the ancient Chinese. The Chinese form of the abacus is that most familiar today, consisting of beads on a wire counting frame, and it is still used in parts of the Far East for commercial arithmetic. In England the abacus took the form of a table divided into strips by lines on which counters were placed. The use of the abacus was necessary because of the awkwardness of Roman numerals, and it was possible to use it for calculation in a completely mechanical way, and without any real knowledge of arithmetic.

In competition with the use of Roman figures and the abacus, our 'Arabic' numerals were of Hindu origin. They were introduced into Europe through Spain by the Moors in the eighth or ninth century A.D. In A.D. 825 Abu Ja'far Mohammed Ben Musa, surnamed 'The Native of Khiva' (al-Khowarazmi), wrote a widely used arithmetic book which was translated into Latin in the twelfth century under the title 'Liber Algorismi de Numero Indorum'. From the corrupt form of the author's surname in this title the term 'algorism' was applied to written calculations using the Arabic numerals. In England, the algorists did not displace the abacists until the end of the sixteenth century, when the term 'counter caster' was a contemporary description of a clumsy calculator.

The first machine for performing the four fundamental operations of arithmetic was invented by Blaise Pascal in 1642, to assist his father, a Customs official. It could be used for money calculations to six figures in francs, and included dials for sous and deniers. In 1671 Leibniz improved Pascal's machine and included a mechanism to carry out multiplication directly. Leibniz commended his machine for scientific as well as com-

3

mercial arithmetic, and it is likely that the development of arithmetical machines was stimulated by a large volume of computation being generated, particularly in astronomy, by the introduction into science of the mathematical theories of Galileo and Newton and their successors. As Leibniz said of his machine: 'the astronomers surely will not have to continue to exercise the patience which is required for computation. It is this that deters them from computing or correcting tables, . . . working on hypotheses, and from discussions of observations with each other. For it is unworthy of excellent men to lose hours like slaves in the labour of calculation, which could be safely relegated to someone else if the machine were used.'

Leibniz's optimism was somewhat premature for his machine was none too reliable, and it was not until the nineteenth century that satisfactory calculating machines were made. This line of development has culminated today in the electrically-driven desk calculators which are widely used for commercial and scientific arithmetic. Towards the end of the same century, in 1876, Kelvin devised his 'Tidal Analyzer' which was a machine for predicting the tides; he commended it in much the same terms as Leibniz as 'substituting brass for brain in the great mechanical labour of calculating'. Kelvin's analyzer simulated the movement of the tides by combining mechanisms performing analogous movements. It was followed by the development of a family of 'analogue computers', which nowadays operate electronically and find their principal applications in engineering.

In using an analogue computer, the problem to be solved is arranged as a model in which the behaviour of the component parts of, say, the engineering system under study is mimicked by that of electronic computing units. There is a close correspondence between the model and its physical counterpart, which makes it easy to translate measurements and ideas from one to the other, but the method has practical limitations. Thus:

(a) The accuracy is low, partly because of the difficulty of setting and maintaining the electrical circuits and partly because the computing units have design limitations

(b) Problems take a considerable time to set up, during which time the computer cannot be used for other work

(c) Since each computing unit introduces errors, the model should use as few units as possible, but minimisation takes time and effort and may diminish the analogy with the real system

(d) The computing units are accurate only over a limited range and the calculations must be scaled to stay within limits.

For these reasons, particularly the first, analogue computers have not found application in commercial work, where 'digital' machines are universally used.

The fundamental difference between analogue and digital computers is in the methods used to represent numbers. These are illustrated by a car speedometer which indicates speed in analogue terms but distance digitally. Thus, in analogue machines numbers are represented by the magnitude

4

of some measurable quantity, for example the strength of an electric current. In digital computers separate indicators are used for each digit in the number, which allows the precision to be increased to any required degree by enlarging the machine to allow it to handle more digits in each number. Thus, typical analogue computers operate with 3 to 4 digit precision, whereas digital computers commonly work with 10 to 12 digit numbers.

The nineteenth century saw also the first attempt to construct a digital computer. Charles Babbage, recognising that the mathematical and scientific tables of his time contained numerous errors, devised a machine —his Difference Engine—which could calculate these tabulations and also print them automatically, thereby avoiding errors due to careless typesetting and imperfect proof reading. This machine he invented in 1812 and began to construct with government support. In 1863 a model of the Difference Engine was used by the Registrar General to calculate the life tables on which much insurance work was based. In 1833 Babbage conceived the idea of an even more automatic machine—his Analytical Engine—which would be able to execute a long sequence of operations under automatic control and so to perform any kind of calculation whatever. The operation of the automatic control was to be directed by a string of perforated cards, a method which had been invented in France a century earlier for the automatic control of silk looms, and from which the Jacquard loom developed. The Analytical Engine was the first digital computer.

Babbage obtained some £17,000 from the Treasury to support his work but in 1842, with little or no result to show, the Government stopped supporting the project. Babbage's ideas were sound: his failure was due in part to limitations in the engineering techniques available at that time, and in part to the grandeur of his design which was to be able to 'store' 1000 numbers each of 50 digits, to add two 50 digit numbers in one second and to multiply two 20-digit numbers in three minutes. The advantages hoped for from the use of the Analytical Engine were: accuracy, speed and once again, 'economy of intelligence'.

In 1871 Babbage died, having spent much of his fortune and most of his life on the project. His ideas were forgotten, and it was not until 1939 that work on a similar machine, the Automatic Sequence Controlled Calculator, was begun in America in collaboration between the International Business Machine Company and Professor Aiken of Harvard. Aiken has said: 'If Babbage had lived 75 years later, I would have been out of a job.' Aiken's machine was largely mechanical, although driven by electric motors and using electric switches. It operated for more than 15 years and produced a large number of mathematical tables which still find use.

Babbage's Analytical Engine was to have been controlled by perforated cards, and in 1889, Herman Hollerith used the same principle in the first punched-card machines, which he produced to speed the statistical aftermath of an American census. These machines were subsequently developed to a high degree, and were being used on an increasing scale until checked by the general introduction of electronic computers into scientific and commercial work in the late 1950s.

During the last War the need arose to compute artillery firing tables for the American Army, and in 1943 an electronic computer known as ENIAC (from Electronic Numerical Integrator and Computer), was made for this purpose. One of its designers, J. P. Eckert, asked recently whether the computer would have been invented without a war, said: 'I think you certainly would have had computers about the same time. . . . The ENIAC could have been invented 10 to 15 years earlier and the real question is, Why wasn't it done sooner?' His fellow designer, J. Mauchley, replied 'In part, the demand wasn't there . . . people may need something without knowing that they need it'.

In the summer of 1944, J. von Neumann learned of ENIAC and began to work with its designers. Two years later this collaboration culminated in the issue of a seminal report which outlined the design of the modern electronic computer. The most important new idea was that the list of instructions for the computer, that is the program for a calculation, could be stored within it in numerical form and be itself operated upon by the computer just as any other numbers. This made it possible to write much shorter programs for complex calculations, and greatly increased the range and scope of the work that computers could do.

These American ideas were brought to Britain, and the first 'stored-program' computer actually to be completed anywhere in the world was EDSAC, which was built in the mathematical laboratory of the University of Cambridge and began operating in May 1949. The first commercial stored-program computer was built by Eckert and Mauchley: named UNIVAC I, it was delivered to the American Bureau of the Census in 1951, and has recently retired after more than 73,000 hours of operational use. The first computer to be applied to office work was a machine which J. Lyons & Co. built as a modified copy of EDSAC. Lyons Electronic Office, LEO for short, began operating on Christmas Eve 1953, and was not retired from active service until January 1965.

Since these pioneers, computers have increased in size, speed, reliability and range of application, but no fundamentally new principle has been introduced. It is common to speak of 'generations' in computer design, thus:

1st Generation: radio valves and components joined by copper wires.

2nd Generation: transistors and components connected by 'printed circuits'.

3rd Generation: integrated circuits in which transistors, components and connexions are all produced in miniature on a ceramic plate.

4th Generation: entire functional units produced as integrated circuits, called 'large-scale integration' or LSI.

To the user, the electronic technology is immaterial. However, these advances in electronics have produced continual improvements in the speed, reliability and cost of computers. Thus, in 10 years the speed of the fastest machine has increased by 200 times, and the cost of a unit calculation has decreased by 500 times. And, there is no reason to expect this rate of improvement to slacken.

See plates 8 & 9

3 Structure and Function

A.D.P. stands for Automatic Data Processing, that is, the use of automatic machines to derive informative results from primary data by the processes of arithmetic and logic. The term E.D.P.—Electronic Data Processing— is also used, especially in America. Computers are popularly regarded as very fast calculating machines and their use for scientific work occasions no surprise. The account that follows, therefore, concentrates on their use in offices.

In an office, the data of A.D.P. are the basic facts about the daily activities of a business or a government department. These arise in workshops, factories, warehouses, transport depots, local or regional offices and the like, and indicate, for example, how many hours have been worked on what job and by whom, how many items of which kinds have been purchased or delivered, information returned by the public and so on. From these data various arithmetical and statistical processes produce accounting documents such as payrolls and bills, and management information such as performance statistics, progress reports and forecasts.

An automatic data processing system invokes no new principle in dealing with this work. It scores over human operators in speed and accuracy but uses essentially the same processes. In the office a computer functions as a supremely competent but quite un-original clerk, and the analysis of a simple office routine can show what principal parts are required in an A.D.P. system. Thus, a clerk working on a weekly payroll. uses:

(1) An in-tray into which are put reports of data that cause a man's pay to vary from his standard rate; for example, the number of hours of overtime worked, absence due to sickness, changes in tax allowances and so on.

(2) A file of data giving for each man such standing information, as his name, pay number, grade, pay scale and position on it, and such running items as the accumulations of his pay to date, tax and deductions for this or that beneficiary.

(3) His own memory, assisted by a scrap pad, into which he brings for each man in turn the input of variation and filed data so that they can be worked on together.

(4) His arithmetical skill, supplemented by a ready reckoner or a simple adding machine with which he performs the calculations that produce the pay from the input and the filed data.

(5) An out-tray from which, having computed the pay and entered it on pay-sheets, and pay-slips, he despatches the results.

(6) A book of rules which regulates the entire process.

An A.D.P. system doing the same payroll would do it in essentially the same way and would require the same six functional units, namely:

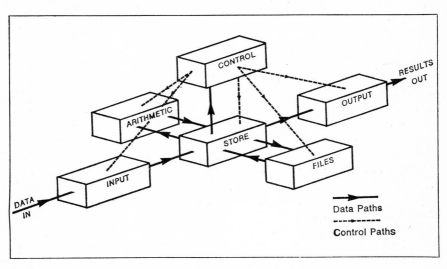

Fig. 1   The Parts of an A.D.P. System

(1) An INPUT unit to take in variation reports and convert them into the electrical impulses that represent data.

(2) A FILE store which commonly consists of magnetic recordings.

(3) A STORE—sometimes called a memory—which can absorb and hold the data taking part in the calculation and give them up as required.

(4) An ARITHMETIC UNIT to perform arithmetical and simple 'logical' operations—for example, comparing.

(5) An OUTPUT unit to accept data from the Store and print it.

(6) A PROGRAM of instructions (rule book), which details the sequence of operations: the program is held in the store, and the CONTROL UNIT draws the instructions from the store one by one, decodes them and sets in train whatever machine operations are necessary to obey them.

The way in which these parts are linked is shown in Figure 1. Data enter the Input and pass to the Store, where they are held until, with other data drawn from the Files, they are worked on in the Arithmetic Unit and the results sent to the Output. All this is closely regulated by the Control Unit, under the complete direction of the instructions in the program, which it draws from the Store. The heart of a large A.D.P. system is called the 'Central Processing Unit' (CPU) or 'Main Frame'; it includes the arithmetic unit, the store and the control unit. Surrounding it are a dozen or more 'Peripheral Units' for dealing with input, output and files. The CPU is an electronic equipment consisting of many thousands of transistors and other electrical devices; it typically occupies three or four large steel cabinets and consumes two or three kilowatts of power, which it draws from the electric mains.

The peripheral units are electrically driven mechanisms in which pieces of paper, card, or magnetic tape are moved about in order to have data recorded on them or replayed. These mechanical devices each have a small amount of electronic control gear, but are noisier, less reliable, slower, dirtier and more power-consuming than the wholly electronic central processor. The total power consumption of a large A.D.P. system might amount to 20 or 30 kilowatts, all of which is eventually dissipated as heat that has to be removed by ventilating fans assisted by refrigeration. All this represents a formidable amount of electronic and mechanical equipment, but its users need no detailed engineering knowledge of how it works—any more than a television viewer needs to understand the workings of his receiver.

To demonstrate how an A.D.P. system tackles a clerical process it is simplest to take a concrete example, say posting a stores ledger, see Figure 2. The ledger is recorded on magnetic tape (Chapter 5) and consists of a file listing for each item in the stores its identification code, the quantity in stock, the maximum permissible stock, the minimum permissible stock, the average cost, and any similar information required for efficient management. This information is recorded in sequence, for example, in item code number order, to make it easy to find the record appropriate to any particular item. The object of posting the ledger is to bring it up to date in terms of the transactions—the issues and receipts of stores—that have taken place since the last posting.

The store transactions are recorded by the store-keeper, and have to be put into a form that a machine can read. For this purpose we will assume that the details of each transaction are entered to coded form on a single punched card (Chapter 4). The first step is to put these transactions into the same sequence as the records are held on the ledger; this is achieved by sorting them by their item codes, which can be done separately by machine in ways that need not concern us here. Figure 2 shows diagrammatically the central processor with at top right the old ledger recorded on magnetic tape and at the top left the sorted pack of punched cards recording the transactions. At bottom right is the reel of magnetic tape on which the newly-posted ledger will be recorded and at bottom left a printed report on matters of interest. There are, thus, four items of peripheral equipment—two magnetic tape units (for the old and the new ledger files), one punched card reader (for the input of transaction data) and one printer (for the output of reported results).

The first step is to place in the store of the central processor the program which has been written to control this ledger posting. The program is recorded on a pack of punched cards which is placed in the card reader,

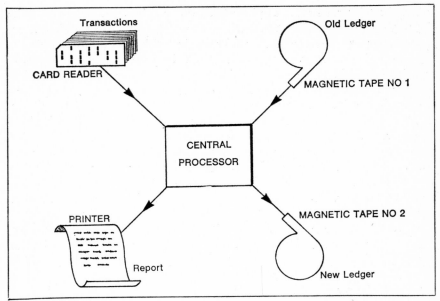

Fig. 2 Ledger Posting by A.D.P.

the operator presses a control button, the reader starts and the program is read and recorded in the store as a pattern of magnetic 'marks' (Chapter 6). The program cards are then removed from the reader and the 'transaction' cards put in. Once this has been done, the operator presses another button to transfer control to the stored program.

The program begins by starting magnetic tape unit No. 1 to read and copy into the store the first record from the old ledger. It then instructs the punched-card reader to read the first transaction card and inspects its item number to decide whether it is the same as that of the first ledger item. If so, that transaction applies to that ledger item. The next step is to inspect the transaction code to determine whether it was an issue or a receipt. Assuming, for example, that it was an issue, the central processor inspects the quantity recorded on the transaction card and subtracts this from the total quantity read from the old ledger. The next transaction cards are then read one by one to determine whether they are further transactions for the same ledger item. When they are, the program proceeds for each as before. When the first transaction card for a different item is reached the data on that card are kept in suspense in the store while the data from the old ledger, now revised in terms of the first and any subsequent cards, are entered as the first item on the new ledger tape. If there has been no transaction for any item its old ledger entry is simply copied on to the new ledger tape. Then the next item is brought in from the old ledger, inspected to see whether the waiting transaction applies to it or not, and so on. When the last transaction card has been read, the old ledger tape is run on to its end, the data relating to items for which there have been no transactions being simply copied on to the new ledger tape. This process is shown diagrammatically by the flow chart in Figure 3.

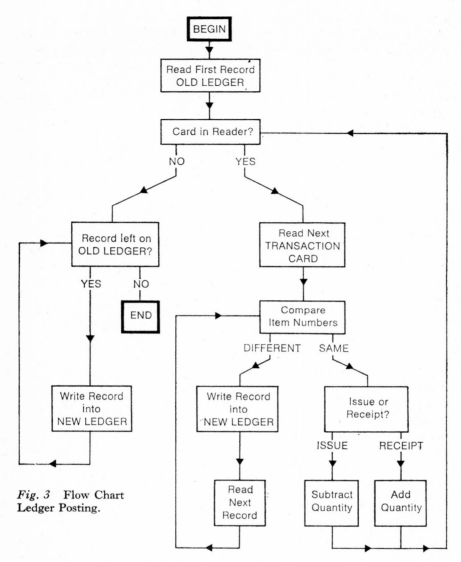

Fig. 3 Flow Chart
Ledger Posting.

So far, no reference has been made to the printer or to the reports which it might produce. The object of posting the ledger is not only to acquire an up-to-date version on the new ledger tape, but also to enable the stores manager to decide which items to re-order and which are overstocked. For this purpose other steps can be included in the program which, for example, after handling the last transaction affecting a particular item, inspect the total quantity shown as remaining in store to determine whether or not this is below the minimum stock, and if so to print out the item number, minimum stock as recorded on the ledger tape and the actual stock, so that the manager can order some more. Similarly, if a new receipt took the stock over the maximum stock quantity recorded on the ledger tape, this also might be reported so that future orders could be delayed to

11

avoid excessive stock-building.

Again, it would be feasible to record on the ledger tape for each item the date of its last transaction and to inspect this each time the ledger were posted to decide which items had had no transactions during some specified preceding period, so that these were brought to notice to allow the manager to consider whether they were becoming obsolete and might be disposed of; or at least whether they might be kept in the more inaccessible parts of the store. A report should be made for only those items which call for some action. Those that call for no action, because, say, their stock is between the minimum and maximum levels or because they are in frequent demand, should not appear on the report; this mildly comforting information can be safely left within the A.D.P. system.

In the example described, it was necessary to sort the transaction cards into the same order as records were held on the old ledger tape. This was because on a tape the ledger records are necessarily held in sequence, and it would be inefficient to run the tape backwards and forwards to match transactions in whatever order these happened to occur. There are, now, ways in which ledgers may be kept on a magnetic material in which any record can be found at random, and by using these it is possible to avoid sorting the transaction cards. One such method uses magnetic disks which rotate continuously at 3,000 r.p.m. so that the whole ledger can be read once each revolution, and any one item can be found with an average delay corresponding to one-half of a revolution, i.e. 0·01 sec. When such files are used the store-keeper can send in his transaction data directly as he issues and receives stores, by using a teleprinter connected to the computer input over a telephone line. The manager of the store also can have a teleprinter and use it to get on-demand answers to his questions about any item. These methods of storing files are discussed below (Chapter 5) but, although important, they affect the details rather than the principles of the way in which computers set about processing data. Again, in scientific work (Chapter 9) and in process control (Chapter 11) there are more calculations and less consultation of files, but the methods of handling data through a specified sequence of processes are essentially the same as those described above for office work.

From time to time the newspapers print stories of how a computer has made some glaring mistake, for example, crediting someone's account with £10,000 instead of £10, or paying a farmer a guarantee cheque made out quite correctly, but foolishly, for £0-0p. Such stories warm the heart, when we reflect on our own fallibility and especially if we feel our job to be threatened by the computer. Computers can produce incorrect results in three main ways.

(a) The input data may be wrong, either because an error was made in recording it, or because it has been wrongly transcribed. With incorrect data even perfect processing must give an incorrect result; the Americans call this a G.I.G.O. system—garbage in, garbage out.

(b) The computer's program may be wrong, for example, because the programmer did not appreciate the full circumstances of the case, or because he made a logical mistake through faulty analysis, or because of copying or transcription errors in writing the program down and preparing it for feeding into the computer.

(c) The computer develops a mechanical or electrical fault which causes it to corrupt the data, the program or the results.

The first kind of errors are tackled by checking all the processes of preparing the input data (see Chapter 4). The second group of errors present difficult problems, and what is called the 'de-bugging' of progams is a painstaking business of analysis and test. The third group of errors can in part be detected by apparatus built into the computer itself, and are also guarded against by checking processes incorporated in the program: thus all the usual accountancy checks of balancing and cross-footing can be applied.

4 Input and Output

ANYONE coming new to computers is understandably puzzled by the contrast between the clumsy methods used for the input of data and the advanced techniques used elsewhere. In most A.D.P. systems data are laboriously recorded by punching holes in pieces of paper or cardboard which are then fed to the computer. In human clerical systems data are more elegantly exchanged by speaking and writing, but the automatic recognition of speech and handwriting by machines poses severe technical problems, largely because both are generated with very few restraints. People speak with varying loudness and speed, and with different accents and vocabularies. They write with great individuality, and present their information in many different ways. Machines are much less tolerant of these variations than men are, partly because to be economic they must apply rather simple criteria, but mainly because the mental processes involved in the recognition of patterns, and so in the comprehension of speech and writing, are little understood.

Some progress is being made with the design of devices that recognise a small group of spoken words, usually the decimal numerals and a few control words, but they are not in general use. Rather more progress has been made with reading machines, and numbers of these are now used by the banks to read numerical data from cheques. In this application the engineering problems have been simplified by limiting the machines to dealing with specially-printed documents of standard sizes on which the data are confined to a well-defined 'coding line', are set out in a carefully specified fashion, and appear in a print font designed for machines to read. This last requirement clashes with human standards for clear and elegant type, as the examples in Figure 4 illustrate.

Two methods of reading are in use. In the first, the document is illuminated and the reflected light is focussed onto photocells. This method is known as optical character reading (O.C.R.). It offers the possibility of dealing with ordinary printed material but is disturbed by the presence of dirt, or over-marking by signatures, endorsements or checking ticks. The second method is magnetic ink character recognition (M.I.C.R.), which uses an ink containing oxides of iron which can be magnetised and read like a magnetic tape. Dirt and superimposed marks are rarely magnetic and do not confuse the reading machine.

The mechanical handling of separate pieces of paper itself poses difficult technical problems which limit the speeds of O.C.R. and M.I.C.R. machines; these, in 1971, lie in the range 100 to 1,500 documents per

14

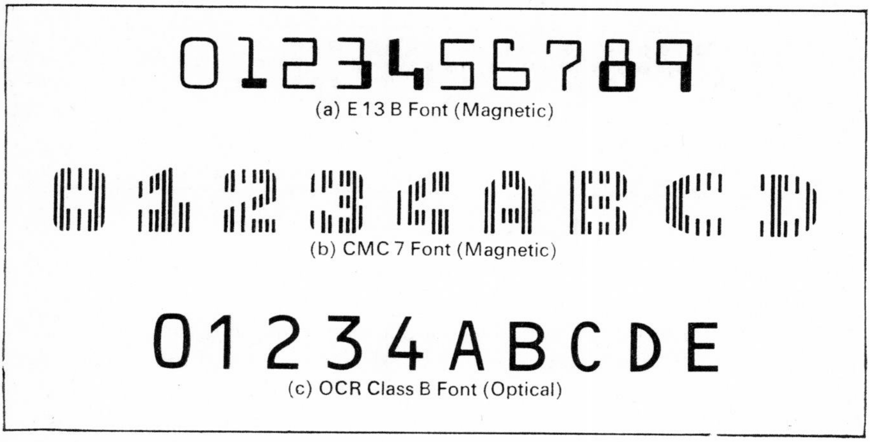

(a) E 13 B Font (Magnetic)

(b) CMC 7 Font (Magnetic)

(c) OCR Class B Font (Optical)

Fig. 4 Machine Fonts (Enlarged)

minute. Some machines read only one line on the document, as for example on cheques, others are designed to read from the whole document. Data input speeds range from 500 to 2,000 characters per second, depending on how many characters are read from each document.

If the reading of print is difficult, the reading of handwriting is much more so, and attention has been mainly directed to reading handprinted numerals or simple marks. Some control can be exercised by requiring writers to confine their entries to printed 'boxes' and to use guiding marks printed in them. It is much easier to recognise the presence or absence of a simple mark in a specified place than to identify a numeral or a letter and methods of 'mark sensing' or 'mark scanning' are attractive for such applications as census enumeration, job recording in workshops, stock-taking and meter reading. Their input speeds also are limited by the mechanics of handling paper to about 1,500 documents per minute.

A familiar way of recording data is by operating a keyboard like a typewriter's and this is the method most commonly used in A.D.P. systems at present. The speed is limited by human fingers to about 2 or 3 characters per second, and for large amounts of data it is usual to use the keyboard to pre-record the data in a coded form which is easy for machines to read later at a much higher speed. The common forms of coding use punched paper tape, punched cards or magnetic tape.

The paper tape used in A.D.P. is about $\frac{3}{4}$ in. to 1 in. wide and is supplied in reels of about 1,000 ft. of tape. Data are recorded by punching rows of round holes across the width of the tape. The pattern of holes in each row represents one character in code and ten such rows are perforated per inch of tape. Various codes are in use and tapes may have five, six, seven or eight holes per row. Figure 5 shows a piece of tape punched according to a seven-hole code. Paper tape is read by illuminating it and using small photocells to detect the holes by the light which comes through. Typical reading speeds are 500 to 2,000 characters per second.

When punching data into tape, it is essential to check for transcription

15

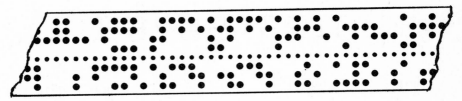

Fig. 5 7-Track Punched Paper Tape

errors. Experience shows that punch operators make two or three errors per 1,000 characters punched, and these would cause unacceptable confusion when reading tape at 1,000 characters per second, for 2 or 3 errors would enter the computer every second. The method of checking is for a second operator to repeat the transcription. She takes the tape produced by the first operator and the documents from which it was prepared and places this tape in a machine called a verifier. This reads the first operator's tape and compares it character-by-character with what the second operator is trying to enter from a keyboard. If the original tape and the keyboard setting agree, the character is punched into a second 'verified' tape. When they differ, the keyboard locks automatically and the verifying operator has to decide which is wrong. She then unlocks the keyboard and enters the correct character into the verified tape. It is common sense to use differently coloured papers for the original and the verified tapes; for example, the original tape may be red for danger and the verified tape white for purity.

Punched cards are of various kinds, of which the most common measures $3\frac{1}{4} \times 7\frac{3}{8}$ ins. and is divided lengthwise into 80 columns; see Figure 6. Each column has 12 positions where rectangular holes may be punched. Usually the pattern of holes punched into one column represents one character, but data can be packed more densely where the range of variation is small; for example, to indicate sex. The remarks about the need to verify paper tape apply equally to punched cards and the method is basically the same. Punched cards are read optically in the same way as paper tape. Reading speeds of up to 2,000 cards per minute are possible, although 600 cards per minute is more typical; at this speed and with 80 characters per card, a card reader feeds data into an A.D.P. system at 800 characters per second, which is at much the same speed as paper tape.

Many different machines are available for handling punched cards; for example, they can be sorted or compared, two packs can be 'merged' by interleaving their cards after comparison, and the whole or specified parts of the data in the cards can be listed, totalled or tabulated. Before the development of computers assemblies of punched card machines were the principal means of data processing; but each machine advanced the process by only a few steps and it was necessary to take many bites at the cherry.

A relatively recent development is the direct entry of data from keyboards onto magnetic tape. The simplest method uses a tape which moves one space at a time, and on which characters are recorded at a relatively wide spacing. After verification, this low-density tape is read into the com-

16

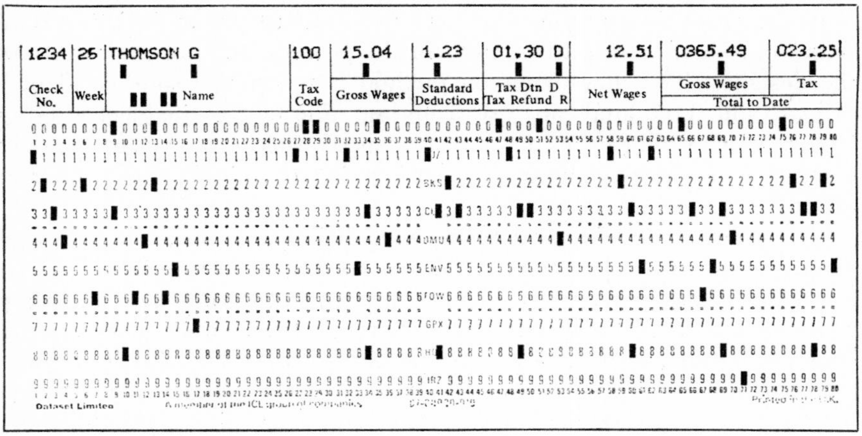

Fig. 6 80-column Punched Card

puter at a rate of about 30,000 char./sec. and its data are transferred to a file tape (Chapter 5). In a more complex approach, several keyboards are connected to a small auxiliary computer which accepts their input and records it on a file tape. Compared with paper-tape or punched-card input these magnetic tape methods offer advantages in terms of speed and noise, and no paper dust is produced. Data usually arise at points remote from an A.D.P. system. It is easy enough to record it where it arises and transport the documents or paper tape or punched cards by van or by post, but when time is important, data can be sent by a line or radio communication channel. This is known as 'data transmission' to distinguish it from plain-language telegraphy, the principal difference being that fewer transmission errors can be tolerated in data transmission since computers have less commonsense than men. Much ingenuity has been applied to the design of codes and equipment to minimise data transmission errors and it is now possible to reduce them to less than one error per million characters transmitted, except when the channel is obviously faulty. The Datel services of the Post Office offer a range of facilities, thus:

Service	Line	Maximum speed Characters per second*
100	Telex	7
100	Private Telegraph	14
200	Public Telephone	25
600	Public Telephone	75
2400	Public Telephone	150
2400	Private Circuit	300
48K	Wideband circuit	6000

*Assumes 8 code elements (bits) per character.

17

It is much easier to produce an effective output from an A.D.P. system than to produce an effective input, for the process is under the control of the designer. The most common method is to operate some kind of a printer, and three kinds are worth noting. The first is the electric typewriter, which produces output at a slow speed—perhaps 10 characters per second—and is principally used either for the control of the computer or for answering occasional enquiries.

The second kind of printer prints a whole line at a time, using a row of hammers to strike the paper against revolving type-wheels or against a moving chain carrying type faces, with an inked ribbon or a carbon paper interposed. The speeds achieved range from about 300 to 2,000 lines per minute, in up to 160 printing positions per line, 1,000 lines per minute being typical; at this speed and with an average of, say, 90 characters per line, the output rate is 1,500 characters per second. To put this more vividly, the whole Bible—Old and New Testaments—could be printed in about 40 minutes. These printers can handle stationery interleaved with carbon paper to take up to six copies simultaneously, the stationery can be pre-printed with standard headings and the printer instructed to skip rapidly over blank paper or between forms.

The third kind of printer displays the characters to be printed on a cathode-ray tube, rather like a television screen. An optical image of the display is focused into a revolving electrified drum where it produces an electric image which is then used to transfer pigment to paper. The process bears the trade name Xerography and is used for copying documents. Xerographic printers have fewer moving parts than hammer printers and so can operate faster. One commercial model operates at 3,000 lines per minute, at which speed it could print the entire Bible in 13 minutes. As well as printing the output data it is also possible by the optical projection of a transparency to print the 'form' on which the data are to appear, and the transparency can be changed automatically to select any of a number of alternative forms. It is also possible to take a microfilm copy of the cathode-ray tube display while printing. The disadvantages of this method of printing are that it is limited to a single copy, and that it cannot skip more rapidly over blank paper, which reduce its apparent advantage in speed over the hammer printers.

Where a printed copy—hard copy—is not required the output can be displayed on the television-type screen of a cathode-ray tube. A typical display can present up to 2,000 characters on its screen, and write them there at a rate set by the Datel Service used to connect it to the computer. Usually the unit is associated with a typewriter-like keyboard for the input of data and the whole is known as a Visual Display Unit, or VDU. The Post Office's speaking clock TIM answers enquirers by selecting pre-recorded phrases, and the same principle can be used to provide a spoken output from an A.D.P. system. For example, the New York Stock Exchange has installed a computer to record information about its transactions, and subscribers to this service can, by dialling codes on their telephones, interrogate the computer about current facts relating to particular stocks. The computer searches its files, locates the required information and puts together a set of recorded standard phrases to produce a spoken answer. Entire speech phrases need not be pre-recorded, for a computer can synthesise the output required by generating and combining the basic sounds of speech in any specified language.

For scientific use, it is sometimes more convenient to graph results than to tabulate them. Automatic graph-plotters are available which do this with a precision that is limited by errors in the printing of the graph paper rather than by the plotting machine. Graphed results can also be displayed for direct viewing on the screen of a cathode-ray tube, and methods have been devised for presenting three-dimensional plots in isometric form.

A large A.D.P. system may employ several input and several output devices all working simultaneously and independently to handle large flows of data and results.

See plates 2, 3, 4, 10, 11

5 Files

THE amount of data which is recorded on files and consulted during the course of clerical work is often much larger than that which comes in as input or leaves as output. It is, therefore, important that filed data should be available to the computer at faster rates than input or output data. At present, magnetic recording of some kind is used to hold all file data in A.D.P. systems.

The most common method uses magnetic tapes which are basically the same as those used for sound recording in dictation machines or for domestic entertainment. For A.D.P., the tape is a ribbon of plastic material, usually $\frac{1}{2}$ in. wide and a few thousandths of an inch thick, and it carries on one side a thin coating of a plastic varnish containing oxides of iron. The tape is supplied and stored on reels which hold from 1,000 to 3,600 feet of tape. The reels are about 10 in. in diameter and are usually driven by electric motors at a tape speed of 100 inches per second (about $5\frac{1}{2}$ m.p.h.). The oxide-coated surface rubs against a 'read/write head' which consists of a group of small electromagnets by means of which the data are recorded (written) and replayed (read). The motors are provided with elaborate automatic controls for ensuring that the tape moves at a steady speed, and for starting or stopping it in a few thousandths of a second.

The method of recording data on magnetic tape is analogous to that used on punched paper tape—the spots of magnetisation on the magnetic tape corresponding to the holes in the punched paper tape. As we have no sense organ that responds to magnetism it is not possible to say by simple inspection whether or not a magnetic tape carries data; some people find this fact faintly mysterious, but it causes no difficulty in practice. The speeds of a punched paper tape and of a magnetic tape are both about 100 in. per second, but the magnetic tape transfers its data to and from the computer at a very much higher rate because it is possible to pack spots of magnetisation much more closely together than holes in a paper tape. Each inch of punched paper tape carries ten rows of code holes, equivalent to ten characters, whereas one inch of magnetic tape may carry 200 to 1,600 rows of magnetic spots or characters. Hence, the speeds at which data are read from or written onto magnetic tape are 20 to 160 times faster than for paper tape, namely 20,000 to 160,000 characters per second.

On most magnetic tapes each character is recorded as a pattern in a 'row' across the tape with nine positions where magnetic spots may be registered. One of these is reserved for a checking signal and the presence or absence of a magnetic spot in the remaining eight positions allows the use of $2^8 = 256$ different patterns and this is enough to cover the letters of the alphabet, the decimal digits, some punctuation and other symbols. When only numerical data have to be represented it is necessary only to distinguish between the ten decimal digits, and four magnetic spots are then sufficient, for these provide for $2^4 = 16$ different characters, it is then possible to pack two independent decimal digits into each row, which means that the rates of data transfer measured in characters per second are doubled. It is possible to pack numerical data even more closely by using the binary system of numbers (Chapter 6). Thus each spot is sufficient to represent one of the two binary digits 0 and 1. Then, for a magnetic tape recorded with nine spots per row, each row represents nine binary digits and a rate of transfer of, say, 150,000 rows per second will correspond to 1,350,000 binary digits per second, more usually, the tape will record two decimal digits per row and thus give a transfer rate of 300,000 decimal digits per second. Faster tapes have speeds of 150 inches per second and a recording density of 1,600 rows per inch, which gives a data transfer rate approaching 500,000 decimal digits per second.

Data are usually transferred to and from tape in chunks, known as 'blocks', which may consist of anything from a few hundred to a few thousand characters. The tape may be started and stopped between blocks to allow the computer to process the data in the block. It takes time, however little, to start and stop a magnetic tape and so a certain amount of blank space has to be left between blocks of data to provide room for the tape to accelerate and decelerate. This blank space, known as the 'inter-block gap', is typically about one inch long. It is obviously desirable to make the blocks of data as long as possible in order to avoid wasting tape. For example, a block of 5,000 characters recorded at a density of 556 characters to the inch would occupy nine inches of tape and when this is followed by an inter-block gap of 1 in. approximately 10% of the tape is wasted. If, however, the size of the data block were reduced to 556 characters occupying only 1 in. and followed by an inter-block gap also of 1 in., then 50% of the tape would be wasted. Why then is the size of the block not increased indefinitely? The reason is that a part of the computer's store corresponding to the block size has to be set aside to receive a block's worth of data; indeed in high-speed processing it may be necessary to have two such areas in alternate use to keep the process going. The larger the block size, the larger the space in the central store that has to be reserved and space in the store is a very expensive commodity which is usually scarce in an economically designed A.D.P. system.

In practice a compromise is struck between the increased costs of tape and of the time to run it when block lengths are short, and the increased cost of the central store when block lengths are long. The amount of tape wasted in inter-block gaps can be reduced by reducing the starting and stopping times of the tape, but this sets very difficult engineering problems when the times are already measured in thousandths of a second. The speed of the tape is not particularly high but the acceleration involved in starting and stopping it in 3 or 4 thousandths of a second is quite substantial, thus the peak acceleration may approach 100 g, and this puts enough strain on the tape to distort or break it.

Another difficulty is that the electro-magnets of the read/write head usually rub on the magnetic oxide coated surface of the tape, and if they are lifted off it in riding over a small particle of dust the recording in that area may be missed. It is, therefore, important that magnetic tape systems operate in reasonably dust-free atmospheres, and smoking is forbidden in some computer rooms. Again, the plastic material of the tape is affected by changes in temperature and humidity and air conditioning is usually necessary.

The questions are sometimes asked—How permanent is the recording of data on magnetic tape? Can it, for example, be used for archival purposes? The answer is that no-one knows from direct experience, because magnetic recordings have not been in use for very long. However, there is no technical reason for supposing that recordings on magnetic tape should not last for a few years at least and this is usually much longer than they are required to last without being re-copied in the ordinary course of processing. The method of amending, or bringing up to date, a magnetic file is not to alter or to insert or delete items, but to re-copy the file completely with whatever changes are needed.

Magnetic tape files have the disadvantage of 'serial access', that is all the preceding records on the tape have to be read in series to reach a wanted record near the end of the reel. This takes minutes rather than seconds, for it typically takes 4 to 5 minutes to read or write a full reel of tape and one minute or so to rewind it. In some applications it is essential to be able to reach any record—chosen at random out of the whole file—in less than a second, and this facility, if cheap enough, would be useful in almost every application. The serial access of magnetic tapes is not wanted, it is accepted because tapes are still cheaper than 'random access' devices. However, the technology is developing rapidly and the economic balance is moving away from tapes. There are three main kinds of random access device, all magnetic, namely disks, drums and cards. Development along these lines could bring considerable changes to the methods of working A.D.P. systems, for example, by obviating the need to sort input data.

Magnetic disk stores consist of a metal disk perhaps 2 to 3 ft. in diameter which revolves continuously on an axle; the flat faces of the disk are coated with iron oxides and used for magnetic recording in exactly the same way as magnetic tape. The records are arranged as concentric rings or 'tracks' of magnetic spots, and are written and read by a head which is moved radially across the disk to 'select' the wanted track. If the head is already on the correct track then all the data recorded on that track are available in the time required for the disk to revolve once. Usually the disks turn at 3,000 r.p.m. completing one revolution in 1/50th second, often written as 20 milliseconds (1 millisecond = 1/1,000th second). This is the maximum waiting time and the average is one-half of it, namely, 10 milliseconds. If the head has to be moved to a different track, this may take about 1/6th second and so add 170 milliseconds to the access time, which brings the total to 180 to 190 milliseconds (say, 1/5th second).

Magnetic disk stores differ in detail but in most of them several disks—

up to 72—are mounted on a common spindle and revolve together. Each disk has two read/write heads, one for each surface, and between them they offer access to any of up to 700 million characters in less than 1/5th second. A large A.D.P. system can have several such disk stores connected to it, to increase the size of the 'file' to say 3,000 million characters—but the cost is substantial. Smaller disk stores are also available in which individual disks, or groups of up to 11 disks, can be changed at will—like changing a gramophone record. These offer random access to a small file or to manually selected parts of large files. A replaceable disk store of this kind can store up to 100 million characters on each group or 'pack' of disks, and give random access times in the range of 70 to 300 milliseconds. Of course, each disk drive unit can have a library of several alternative disk-packs which an operator can select and mount as required. And, one computer can handle 10 or 20 disk drives simultaneously if this is necessary to enlarge the size of the file.

In some applications the access time of disk stores is too long for efficient operation, and one or more magnetic drums are used. The principle is essentially the same, but the magnetic material is disposed around the curved surface of a metal drum, rather than on the flat face of a disk. Magnetic drums have diameters of about one or two feet, and can offer access times as low as 4 milliseconds, to 2 to 3 million characters. The cost of their higher speed is a lower capacity and a higher price as compared with disks.

A cheaper form of magnetic file with random access uses magnetic cards, which are essentially like short lengths of magnetic tape. The plastic base material is thicker and wider than that used for tape, but the principle is the same. Typically the cards are held in cassettes or magazines of a hundred or two, and mechanical devices enable any chosen card to be extracted automatically from any of a number of magazines, then passed over a read/write head for the transfer of data to or from the card, and finally the card is returned to its magazine. The magazines can be changed to change the file or part of the file available to the machine—rather as reels of tape can be changed on a magnetic tape unit. The larger magnetic card machines offer somewhat similar performance to a magnetic disk file, say access to 500 million characters in $\frac{1}{5}$ second or less.

It is worth reverting to the illustration used in the previous chapter. Thus, using magnetic tape an A.D.P. system can hold the equivalent of 7 complete Bibles on a single reel, and read or write one Bible's-worth of information in less than a minute. A large system may have four or more file tapes working simultaneously and so be reviewing the equivalent of a Bible every few seconds. Using magnetic disks the equivalent of several hundred Bibles could be filed and any verse in any one of these could be found and read in a fraction of a second.

See plates 5 & 6

6 Electronic Arithmetic

IT is at first sight strange that machines *can* perform arithmetic, which we commonly regard as a mental process. In fact the machines do no such thing. In a computer, numbers are represented by electric currents, and to add two numbers together the currents that represent them are passed through a network of wires and switches. The switches are set according to rules which have been derived from the arithmetical rules for addition, and the current that results represents the sum of the two numbers. The computer is not 'doing arithmetic' it is manipulating electric currents. In the same way the movement of the beads of an abacus is not 'doing arithmetic', but can be used to parallel the processes of arithmetic.

The digits 0, 1, 2, 3, . . .9 could be represented by electric currents of increasing strengths. Then, however, the computer would have to distinguish between ten different strengths of current and it is easier in practice to make electric circuits operate reliably when they have to detect only whether the current is 'on' or 'off', and not how strong it is. For the input of data to a computer numbers are represented as patterns of holes in cards or tapes; similarly, patterns of 'current on' and 'current off' represent numbers inside the computer. For example, the absence of a hole might correspond to current off and the presence of a hole to current on; and the same code could then be used to represent numbers inside the computer as in the punched tape or punched card. It turns out that it is simpler to use 'binary' arithmetic.

In binary there are only two digits '0' and '1' instead of the ten of the ordinary decimal scale. Clearly, current off could represent '0' and current on '1'. In decimal numbers the first position or column represents the units, the next the tens, the next the hundreds (10^2), the next the thousands (10^3), and so on. Similarly, in binary numbers the first position represents units, the next the twos, the next the fours (2^2), the next the eights (2^3), the next the sixteens (2^4), and so on. Some decimal numbers and their corresponding binary numbers appear below:

Decimal Number	Binary Number	Decimal Number	Binary Number
0	0	8	1,000
1	1	9	1,001
2	10	10	1,010
3	11	100	1,100,100
4	100	1,000	1,111,101,000
5	101	1,023	1,111,111,111
6	110	1,024	10,000,000,000
7	111	1,025	10,000,000,001

Binary arithmetic follows the same rules as ordinary decimal arithmetic but is less convenient for human use since more digits have to be written and more carries made from one column to the next. An electronic computer using binary carries out numerous rapid operations with simple signals, which makes for simple equipment. In contrast, a man, using the decimal scale, carries out fewer operations with more complex symbols which makes for simpler, slower mental processes.

When adding two single-digit binary numbers each can be either 0 or 1 and there are four cases as below:

Sum of		Result	
First No.	*Second No.*	*Carry to next 'column'*	*Sum in first 'column'*
A	*B*	*C*	*S*
0	0	0	0
0	1	0	1
1	0	0	1
1	1	1	0

This table can be described in words; for example:

(a) S is '0' when A *and* B are the same; and '1' when they differ

(b) C is '0' when A *or* B is '0'; and '1' when A and B are both '1'.

These two statements parallel statements (c) and (d) below which describe the operation of the electric lamp circuit of Fig. 7 namely:

(c) Lamp S is 'off' when switches A and B are set similarly; and 'on' when they differ

(d) Lamp C is 'off' when switch A or B is set to '0'; and 'on' when both switches are set to '1'.

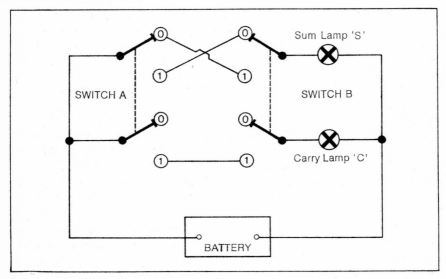

Fig. 7 Binary Adding Circuit

It follows that the electric circuit can be used to indicate the result of adding two binary numbers by setting switches A and B to correspond to digits A and B and reading the results from lamps S and C. This simple illustration shows the direct correspondence between an arithmetic operation, a description in words of its 'logic', and the operation of an analogous electric circuit.

In general, addition involves three digits, namely, A, B, and the digit carried from the previous column. The result can be produced by first adding A to B—producing an initial sum and carry—and then adding this initial sum to the carry from the previous position, to produce the final sum and the final carry. To handle numbers containing more than one binary digit we can use separate adding circuits for each digit position. This is the 'parallel' method and the time required for the addition is only that required to add two single-digit numbers plus a little more to transfer and add in the carries. Alternatively, we can use a single adding circuit and add corresponding pairs of digits of the two multi-digit numbers in succession. This is the 'serial' method and takes longer but is less expensive in equipment: it corresponds to the human method of adding one column at a time, and storing the carry digits temporarily in memory.

In computers, numbers are not represented by continuous electrical currents but by very brief surges or pulses of electric current. These pulses each last a ten-millionth of a second or less and they follow each other at fixed intervals at rates which range in different designs from 100,000 to 10 million pulses per second. The presence of a pulse represents a '1' and the suppression of a pulse when one was due represents '0'.

Subtraction can be done by designing an electric circuit that follows the rules of subtraction, or by adding complements. This is most readily illustrated in terms of decimal arithmetic but the same principles apply to binary. The complement of a decimal number is the difference between it and ten: similarly, the complement of a binary number is the difference between it and two. Thus, the complement of 3 is $(10 - 3) = 7$. If we subtract, say, 3 from 8, the result is 5. The same result is obtained by adding to 8 the complement of 3, and discarding whatever should be carried to the 'tens' column. Thus, the complement of 3 is 7 and $(8 + 7) = 15$, which on discarding the carried '1' leaves the same result as direct subtraction. In binary it is particularly easy to form complements because it simply means changing '0's into '1's and '1's into '0's.

Multiplication can be done by repeated addition: thus to multiply a number by 4, add on itself 3 times. Division can be done by repeated subtraction; thus, to divide a number by 4 subtract 4 from it repeatedly until the result is less than 4 and count the number of subtractions made. In these ways, the four basic operations of arithmetic can all be reduced to addition, and it is only necessary to provide an adding circuit in the computer.

Some computers do not perform their arithmetic in the binary scale but use groups of pulses to represent decimal numbers in the same way as groups of holes or magnetic marks are used on cards and tapes. These pulse groups are then switched according to rules which derive from those for decimal addition. Decimal adding circuits are more complicated than binary ones, but a compensatory saving comes because it is not necessary to use the computer to convert its input and output data to and from the binary scale.

As well as arithmetic operations the central processors of A.D.P. systems perform some simple logical operations such as comparison, sequencing, sorting, selecting. These, however, can be done by arithmetic. For example, to compare two quantities, first express them numerically and then the comparison can be made by subtracting one from the other; if they are the same the answer will be '0', and if they differ the answer will not be '0'. The 'logical' operation of comparison thus reduces to the 'arithmetical' operation of subtraction plus testing the result. Again, quantities can be put into sequence by expressing them numerically and comparing them by subtraction to determine whether they should remain in their present sequence or be interchanged. By repeated interchanges it is possible to put a string of numbers into ascending numerical order. The process of selection is essentially one of comparing quantities in the input data with quantities already stored in the computer and then initiating some appropriate action.

A computer performs its arithmetic or its logical processes with quantities represented by numbers which it draws from its store. The speed of performing the arithmetic is determined in part by the speed with which the electronic switches in the arithmetic circuits can be operated, and in part by the speed with which numbers can be extracted from and returned to the store. The electronic switches operate in a fraction of a ten-millionth of a second and do not at present set the limit, for this is much faster than numbers can be exchanged with the store. It is, therefore, the speed of the store which mainly determines the speed of computers at the present time.

The storage of data is one of the oldest distinctively human practices, as ancient inscriptions testify. Even so, it is one of our more rapidly developing techniques, as new applications make ever higher demands on storage capacity and speed. Magnetic storage is the most popular, and the most common type of high-speed stores uses small rings of a ceramic magnetic material called a ferrite; each ring is about the size of a small letter o and is known as a magnetic core. A core can be magnetised in either a clockwise or anti-clockwise direction, and the alternative directions can be used to represent binary '0' and '1'. The cores are threaded on a rectangular grid of wires at the crossing points and any particular core can be selected for the recording or recovery of data by energising the wires that intersect in it. In a large computer there may be ten million or more cores, and stored items of data can be selected in a time which may be less than a millionth of a second. The speed of arithmetic depends on the time required to obtain two numbers from the store and to return the result to it and therefore exceeds ten million additions per second in the fastest machines.

For arithmetic and for storage it is usual to break the stream of data into chunks of a convenient size; these commonly include about 40 to 50 pulses representing an equal number of binary digits (universally abbreviated to 'bits'). A chunk of 40 bits can represent binary quantities up to a number consisting of forty '1's, i.e. $(2^{40} - 1) = 1,099,511,627,775$. Alternatively, it can be used as 5 groups, or bytes, of 8 bits, each byte representing two decimal digits, when it would represent decimal quantities up to a number consisting of ten '9's, i.e. $(10^{10-1}) = 9,999,999,999$. These chunks of data are rather confusingly known as 'words', and the number of bits in its words—the 'word length'—indicates the precision of the arithmetic performed by a computer. The store is divided into cells or 'locations' each able to hold one unit of data, and each identified by a serial number known as its 'address', by analogy with a postal address. In most machines the data unit is a word (32 to 60 bits) or short-word (16 to 24 bits), but in some it is a byte of 8 bits.

The capacity of the core store ranges from about 1,000 words in very small A.D.P. systems to 500,000 words in large ones; it is an expensive item but not one which can be cut down too severely without handicapping the use of the system. In some machines the cost is cut by using a small amount of fast core store, backed up by a much larger amount of cheaper, slower cores.

See plate 7

Plate 1   *The computer room, Post Office LACES Centre (By courtesy of The Post Office)*

Plate 2   *A visual display
unit (VDU)*
(*By courtesy of Cossor
Electronics Limited*)

Plate 3 From the console typewriter the operator can read a hard copy of the status of the system at the same time that it is displayed on the console. Operator messages are transmitted and instructions can be keyed in.
(By courtesy of IBM United Kingdom Limited)

Plate 4 *A line printer*
(By courtesy of IBM
United Kingdom
Limited)

Plate 5a *A reel of magnetic tape*
(By courtesy of International Computers Limited)

Plate 5b *Removing a reel from its protective storage container and loading a reel onto a tape deck*
(By courtesy of The Post Office)

HWZ 014

Plate 6 *Loading a disk pack onto a disk drive (By courtesy of The Post Office)*

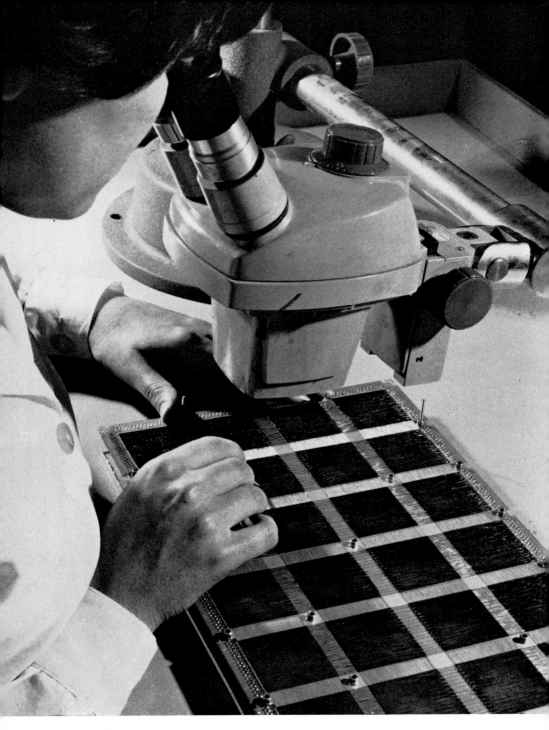

Plate 7   *Visual inspection
of a core store plane,
following threading of the
cores
(By courtesy of The Plessey
Company Limited)*

Plate 8 *An integrated circuit going through the eye of a sewing needle. The needles are size 5; the thread, ordinary 40 gauge sewing cotton*
(By courtesy of Mullard Limited)

Plate 9   *Inserting an
integrated circuit module into
a logic bay
(By courtesy of the Univac
Division Sperry Rand
Limited)*

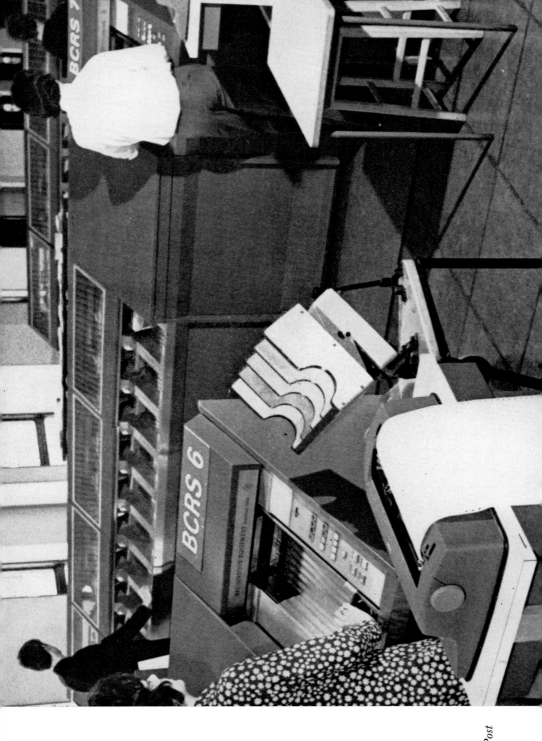

Plate 10 *An OCR reader/sorter (By courtesy of The Post Office)*

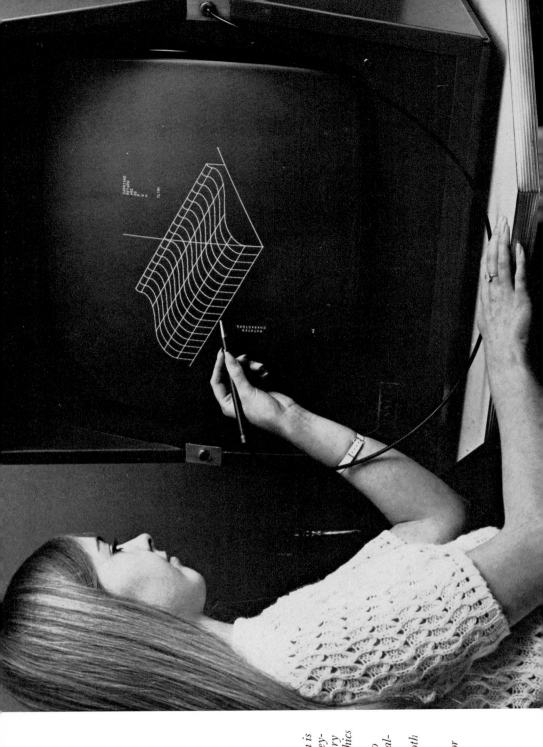

Plate 11   A light pen is
the alternative to a key-
board as method of entry
in this high speed graphics
display system which
enables an operator to
establish two-way, real-
time communication
with a computer in both
alphanumeric and
graphic terms
(By courtesy of Cossor
Electronics Limited)

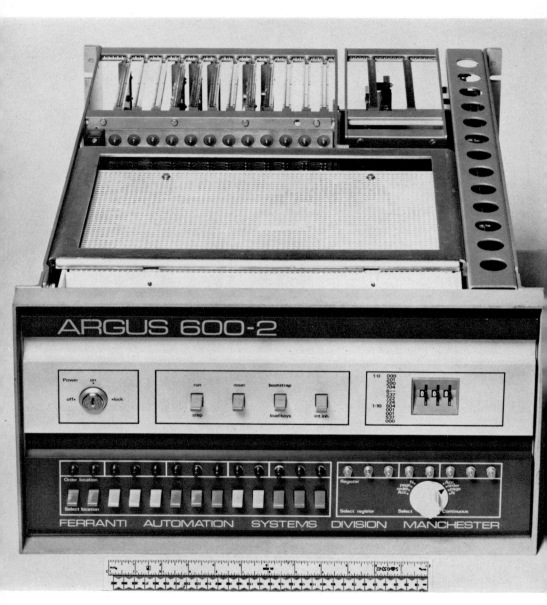

Plate 12   *A small Argus computer*
(*By courtesy of Ferranti Limited*)

7 Overall Control

THE job of the control unit is to co-ordinate the actions of the parts of an A.D.P. system so that they combine to execute the instructions in its program. In considering how the control unit does this it is simplest to begin with the central processor itself and see how the instruction for addition is controlled.

First, what does a computer instruction look like? As stored in the computer it usually consists of a string of bits making up one computer 'word'; and it has two parts which in decimal might for example be 01,2856. The first part of this instruction tells its computer to perform 'Function 01', and in that particular machine 01 might stand for 'Add', with 02 meaning 'Subtract', 03 'Multiply' and so on: unfortunately these codes are different for different machines, according to the whims of their designers. The second part of the instruction gives the 'address' of the 'location' in the store which holds the quantity to be added, that is, the number of the pigeon-hole in which it is to be found. Hence, this whole instruction says: 'Add to whatever is already in the Arithmetic Unit whatever number is in Location 2856 of the store.' Not every instruction needs an address part; for example, the code 00 in the function part might mean 'Reset the Arithmetic Unit to zero', and for this function no address is relevant.

Then, for this computer, the instructions required to add together, say, the numbers in Locations 2856 and 2857 of the store and put the result in Location 3642 are:

00,   meaning: Reset arithmetic unit to zero
01,2856   meaning: Add in the number from Location 2856
01,2857   meaning: Add in the number from Location 2857
05,3642   meaning: Transfer the result now in the arithmetic unit to Location 3642 (supposing that 05 is the code for 'Transfer').

This brief program is one for a computer having a single address-part in its instructions, but computers have been made which have instructions with two, three or even four address-parts. For a three-address machine the program would reduce to:

00,
01,2856,2857,3642

where the second instruction collects the 'operands' (i.e. the quantities to be operated upon) and disposes of the result. Most commercial machines use single-address instructions.

The control unit often operates to a two-beat rhythm. In the first beat it obtains the next instruction from the store and places it in a special single-location store. Computers contain a number of these special-purpose stores. They are usually called registers; for instance, this one might be called the 'Present Instruction Register'. In the second beat the control unit examines the binary digits that make up the instruction and determines which electrical controls to energize in order to initiate the required operation. When the operation has been completed a signal is returned to the control unit, which then proceeds to obtain the next instruction. This rhythm: Obtain and Store, Examine and Obey, repeats until the program has been completed.

Normally the instructions of a program are held in adjacent locations in the store and obeyed in sequence. The address of the first instruction is indicated to the control unit by the computer operator, and it can then calculate the address of the next instruction by adding 1 to the address from which it obtained the instruction now being obeyed. Some instructions allow this strict sequence to be broken, but they have to indicate to the control unit where its next instruction is to come from.

As well as controlling the central processor, the control unit directs the execution of instructions calling for the transfer of data to or from peripheral units, such as card readers, magnetic tapes and printers. These somewhat ponderous mechanisms are very slow compared with electronic operations in the central processor. The control unit deals with them by galvanising them into activity and then turning to another instruction while waiting for them to complete their operation. The other instruction may be one for a fast central-processor operation, or it too may initiate action by another slow peripheral unit or dispose of the results of an earlier peripheral instruction. To allow for this loose-jointed form of operation the peripheral equipments are provided with small individual stores called buffer registers. They empty and fill these buffers at their own pace, and the buffers transfer their contents at very much higher electronic speeds to or from the main store in the central processor. In this way several peripheral devices may be kept operating simultaneously with computing. Peripheral equipments which operate directly connected to the central processor in this way are said to work 'on line': by contrast a printer working independently of the central processor under the control of a magnetic tape previously recorded by the processor would be 'off line'.

However, it is not always possible to proceed with the main program until some slow peripheral unit has disgorged or swallowed some more data, and this limits the extent to which peripheral and central processor operations can be overlapped. A greater degree of overlap can sometimes be arranged by interleaving the activities of several programs which make differently timed demands on the central processor and on the peripheral units. In this 'time-sharing' the several programs appear to proceed simultaneously; however, the central processor can execute only one instruction at a time, and it is more correct to say that the programs run concurrently. Time-sharing offers the possibility of keeping every item of equipment in an A.D.P. system—central processor and peripherals alike—

operating continuously at full speed in the interests of efficiency. This is, however, far from easy to achieve in practice for it demands an unusually harmonious mixture of requirements.

A practical application of time-sharing is in 'real-time' processing. In this the computer processes data as they arise and keeps in time with events in the real world as they occur. An example is airline seat reservation, in which the flight plans of the aircraft available are expressed in digital form, stored inside a computer, and consulted as required by ticket agents as they deal directly with customers' enquiries. To give a good service the ticket agent must be able to interrupt anything less urgent that the computer is doing and have his enquiry dealt with on demand. The enquiry service is available throughout the day but the incidence of enquiries varies considerably so that the computer is more fully occupied at some periods than at others. It is possible to use its spare capacity when enquiries are few by providing it with a 'base-load' program, perhaps an accounting one, which can share the computer with the 'real-time' program for seat-reservation. In this way we can hope to obtain the benefits of high average loading while retaining sufficient capacity for occasional peak demands.

8 On Programming

WE have seen that a computer is set up to do a particular job by placing a program of instructions in its store, and that its control unit draws these instructions one by one and obeys them in sequence. The usual physical form of a program is a pack of punched cards or a reel of punched paper tape, and the program is placed in the computer's store by feeding the cards or tape through one of its input mechanisms. The program consists of a list of instructions, each instruction being a statement in a numerical code, as described in the previous chapter.

A program is prepared by making a thorough analysis of the job to be done, in order to break it down into a sequence of the very elementary steps that computers perform. An example of such a step is: 'Add in the number in Storage Location No. 3967.' For mathematical work this means reducing all calculations, however complicated, to the basic operations of arithmetic and there is a well-developed technique for doing this which is known as Numerical Analysis (Chapter 9). For business work the corresponding process is called 'Systems Analysis' and involves a penetrating investigation into the sources, forms, accuracies and volumes of the primary data, the activities and procedures to which it is subjected and the numbers, forms and distributions of the results required.

A numerical or systems analyst commonly specifies the processes required in graphic form by means of a flow chart, which sets out the sources of data, the courses followed and the operations and interactions that are to take place. Figure 3 is one such chart, and Figure 8 presents another example of part of the flow chart of the office processes relating to the calling up of staff for mass radiography. Next, the flow chart is translated into the appropriate sequence of coded instructions. On a modern computer we can do this in various ways.

Inside the computer the program is stored in binary form and the direct decimal equivalent of this, which is what is punched into the program cards, is known as 'machine code'. The instructions illustrating the previous chapter are in such a machine code. Machine codes are chosen to suit the requirements of engineering design of the computer's electric circuits, which gives them a somewhat abstract structure that makes little concession to the convenience of the programmer. When programming in machine code a programmer has to keep a meticulous running account of what he has placed, or left, in every location in the store of the computer. At every step in the execution of the program he must know exactly where are every instruction, item of data, intermediate or final result, and take care not to

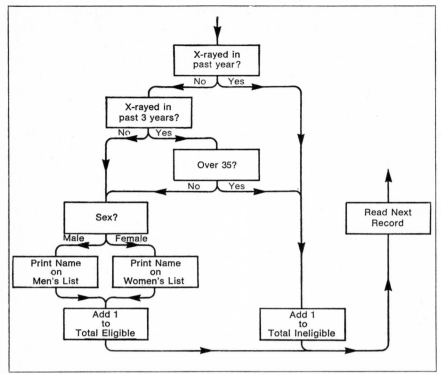

Fig. 8 Flow Chart

mislay, or alter, or erase, or overwrite anything that he will need subsequently. He must also make sure that the numbers taking part in his calculation do not grow too large for his machine to handle, for if they do the higher digits 'drop off the end' and are lost, with serious results. Each of his instructions specifies the actual address of the storage locations concerned. All this makes programming in machine code a task for trained, experienced, patient and meticulous specialists, who are using the code frequently enough to become familiar with it; and it makes machine-code programs very tedious for the less expert to read or understand, and difficult to amend at a later date. The step taken by a computer in obeying a single instruction is much smaller than those natural to human thought. This itself poses problems and makes computer programs unbelievably prolix.

The first simplification of programming came with the introduction of forms of instruction which used letters as well as numbers. These allow mnemonic codes to be devised for the function part of the instructions, e.g. ADD, SUB, MULT, DIV. Then, the address part of the instruction was allowed to refer not to the actual or 'absolute' address, but to a 'relative address' which shows the location of the data being operated upon relative to that of associated items in the same group. No computer can obey such instructions directly. They must first be translated into machine code with the appropriate absolute addresses. Fortunately, this is a process

33

which a computer can do for itself by using a standard program written by its manufacturer especially for this purpose. This translating program is called an 'assembly program' and the mnemonic code used to write instructions is an 'assembly language'. There is usually one instruction in assembly language for each machine code instruction, so the programs are no shorter; but the tedious chores of 'absolute' addressing and keeping track of the contents of all store locations, are both greatly reduced.

The success of assembly languages encouraged the development of even 'higher level' programming languages, which achieved larger amounts of processing for each instructing statement written by the programmer. This reduces the number of logical howlers made by programmers, and makes their programs much easier for others to follow and to check. Each such instructing statement translated into three, five or more instructions in machine code. The first of these languages were known as automatic-programming codes or 'autocodes' and were intended primarily for mathematical work. An example is the BASIC (Beginners All-purpose Symbolic Instruction Code) language devised by Dartmouth College for newcomers to programming. Using this language it is possible to cause two or more quantities A, B, C, etc. to be added together, and the quantity Z to be made equal to the resultant sum. This may be done by writing the instruction:

LET $Z = A + B + C + D + \ldots \ldots$

Similarly we may multiply, divide and subtract by writing:

LET $Z = A * B$ (Multiplication)
LET $Z = A / B$ (Division)
LET $Z = A - B$ (Subtraction)

More complex expressions than these can be written, and the language is mnemonic in that they resemble ordinary algebraic notation. The facility to use symbolic addresses, Z, A, B, C, etc. instead of having to specify actual (absolute) store addresses is a great convenience to the programmer. BASIC, like most other programming languages, requires the programmer to observe certain restrictions, for example, that only capital letters may be used, with certain special symbols such as £, :, /, + and *. The symbol * is used for multiply instead of X in order to allow X to represent a quantity. These restrictions are imposed because they greatly simplify the standard program which has to be written to translate the language into machine code. The translation process is called 'Compiling' and the manufacturer's translating program is called a 'Compiler'. Nevertheless, in spite of its restrictions and conventions, it is possible to learn to write simple programs in BASIC language reasonably well with two or three days training and practice instead of the three to six months or more needed to become proficient in a machine language.

Machine codes, assembly languages and autocodes are each peculiar to one machine or, at best, to a few models in one manufacturers' range of machines. Several programming languages have to be learned to be able to use several different machines, and programmers trained on different machines find it difficult to exchange ideas on programming methods and practices. The next step upwards in the development of programming languages was to produce standard languages, and three in particular have become accepted internationally.

The international programming language for mathematics is known as ALGOL. The name derives from the initial letters *Algo*rithmic *O*riented *L*anguage: an algorithm is a precisely defined procedure for calculating something, an extension of the algorism concept mentioned in Chapter 2. A simple example of an ALGOL statement is:

$$c: = a + b;$$

which makes c equal to the sum of a and b.

Another one is:

$$a: = y \uparrow 2 + 4 \hat{x} z \uparrow 3;$$

which makes a equal to the sum of y^2 and 4 times z^3.

ALGOL is controlled by an international committee and most modern computers will accept programs written in it; that is to say their manufacturers have written ALGOL compilers. For some machines these do not cater for the complete range of facilities offered by ALGOL and unfortunately ALGOL does not standardize the input or output of data. ALGOL is being used increasingly for writing programs, and for the publication of algorithms which demonstrate the solution of some programming problem.

Another, widely used, mathematical programming language is FORTRAN (*For*mula *Tran*slator), which was developed for IBM machines, in certain respects it has less flexibility than ALGOL but most modern computers of all makes now have a FORTRAN compiler. The FORTRAN equivalents of the two ALGOL examples quoted above are:

$$C = A + B$$
$$A = Y ** 2 + 4 * Z ** 3$$

Capital letters only can be used, and ** is used instead of $\uparrow$ to indicate the raising of variables to higher powers.

The international business language is called COBOL from *Com*mon *B*usiness *O*riented *L*anguage. In this it is possible to write in a restricted kind of business English, for example:

COMPUTE NETPAY EQUALS GROSSPAY LESS TAX

Many modern computers are equipped with COBOL compilers but, as for ALGOL, they do not all deal with the full range of COBOL. The compiler programs which have been written tend to produce machine code programs that take up more room in the core store and are slower to operate than corresponding programs written directly in machine code by experienced programmers. However, COBOL is quicker to write than machine code and much easier to understand, and as computers grow larger, faster and cheaper it is becoming cheaper to waste the time of machines than of programmers.

Owing something to FORTRAN and also to COBOL, PL/1 is a language which was designed by IBM to cater for as wide a range of programming applications as possible by combining the facilities of both commercial and scientific high level languages. It has yet to gain wide international acceptance, although compilers are being produced by some other manufacturers. The PL/1 equivalents of the FORTRAN and

COBOL examples quoted above are:

$$C = A + B$$
$$A = Y ** 2 + 4 * Z ** 3$$
$$NET \_ PAY = GROSS \_ PAY - TAX$$

where __ is a break character

The compilers and certain other standard programs supplied by a manufacturer with his computer are known as its 'software'—in contrast to its 'hardware' which is the actual machines and equipment. Software comprises:

(a) operating procedures which help users to feed data into their machines, to organise their working and to put out results

(b) a simple assembly language and assembly program

(c) scientific languages and compilers, e.g. ALGOL

(d) commercial languages and compilers, e.g. COBOL

(e) utility programs for such commonplace jobs as sorting data or transferring it between different parts of the A.D.P. system

(f) a library of standard programs, for example, mathematical routines for calculating such common functions as sine, cosine and logarithm, and standard parts of commercial programs such as routines for P.A.Y.E. or National Insurance deductions.

(g) An Operating System which controls the overall running of the machine and organizes timesharing and the scheduling of programs to make efficient use of the core store and peripherals.

The preparation of the software for a new machine is a difficult and expensive task which requires the best programming brains and a lot of time. Thus the total number of instructions in the software of one major range of commercial computers was estimated to exceed 5 millions and to have grown at an average rate of 60% p.a. over the preceding years. It can cost up to £1 million for a medium-sized machine. Whenever a manufacturer introduces a new computer he has to choose which programming languages his machine shall use. There are already more than a thousand different computer languages and it is greatly to be hoped that the future will see improvements to the internationally standard languages which will make them efficient and universally acceptable: certainly there has been a great duplication of effort.

9 Sums for Scientists

THE modern digital computer has grown out of the work begun by Charles Babbage in 1812 on a simpler type of automatic calculating machine called the 'Difference Engine'. This was completed and used to calculate standard tables by the method of differences which can be illustrated by using it to prepare a table of squares. Thus, the first few entries are:

Number	Square	1st Differences	2nd Differences	3rd Differences
0	0			
		1		
1	1		2	
		3		0
2	4		2	
		5		0
3	9		2	
		7		0
4	16		2	
		9		0
5	25		2	
		11		
6	36			

The third column lists the differences between adjacent squares: the fourth column the differences between these differences and so on. It will be seen that the 2nd Differences all equal 2. Babbage's difference engine prepared a table of squares by first building up the 1st Differences by adding on two each time, and then adding on these differences to build up the squares. Thus to find the next square in the above table, adding 2 to 11 gives the value 13 for the next '1st Difference' and then adding 13 to 36 gives the value 49 for the square of 7.

For cubes the 3rd Differences are the constant ones, and this 'method of differences' can be used for any 'polynomial', which is the mathematician's name for an expression like:

$$y = 5x^4 - 6x^3 + 9x^2 + 8x - 14$$

In this polynomial the 4th differences are constant. A great many of the standard formulae used in mathematical applications are either themselves polynomials or can be closely represented by a polynomial, so the method of differences is of wide application. Babbage's Difference Engine was designed just to add up successive differences, but his later Analytical Engine (like its successor the computer) had wider powers. The method of differences is one illustration of 'numerical analysis', the process of reducing a mathematical calculation to simple arithmetical operations which can be performed automatically and mechanically.

Similar methods of numerical analysis are available for solving sets of simultaneous equations, and for solving differential equations. These latter are most important in science and technology, for they describe the rates and modes of change that occur in physical systems when conditions alter. Comparatively few differential equations can be usefully solved by rigorous methods of mathematical analysis, but step-by-step methods of numerical solution have been developed which can be used with computers.

The use of computers has indeed made it feasible to undertake calculations of much greater magnitude than ever before, for they can complete in a few seconds as much arithmetic as would take a man many more years. Engineers can now calculate the stresses and strains in each individual member of a complex structure such as a bridge or the framework of a large building, taking account of the effects of high winds, and trying out variations in design. In this way a safer yet more economic structure can be designed, since large factors of safety need not be applied blindly to the whole. Here the computer is not doing something the engineer did not previously know how to do, for he must know how in order to program the computer; the computer is, however, allowing him to embark on calculations which would previously have taken far too long to complete.

This particular benefit of the computer is not confined to civil engineers, it is available to technologists, scientists, statisticians, economists, indeed to all concerned with quantitative analysis of any kind. There is, however, a limitation to the use of computers in that errors inevitably creep in, and there are four troublesome sources of error in numerical work.

First, the engineering, economic or physical situation can be described only by idealising and simplifying it and so by omitting some factors. Its mathematical formulation can do no more than represent an hypothesis about some part or aspect of 'reality'. And, usually the same situation can be represented by a variety of theoretical models, more or less accurate.

The second source of errors arises because the evaluation of the adopted model depends on values derived from observations and these will be affected by inaccuracies due to measurement or to sampling.

Third, the formulation of the model will generally involve mathematical operations such as computing sine or logarithmic functions, or integrating, differentiating and so on. These have to be approached numerically by algorithms which have a finite number of steps, and which therefore limit 'infinite' mathematical processes at a point where the level of approximation is judged to be satisfactory. The strict mathematical statement is thus replaced by an approximate numerical one, and the errors involved may become significant when the steps are very numerous. In economic models particularly, the need for large systems of simultaneous equations produces a highly complex computing situation requiring enormous number of calculations.

The fourth source of error derives from the physical limitations of the computer which restrict its precision. Analogue computers are afflicted with electrical disturbances and digital machines can only handle numbers of so many digits. These lead to errors in the performance of each elementary arithmetic operation, and in a large-scale computation there may be millions of such operations. Errors of this kind occur even when the computers are working faultlessly.

The mathematician Norbert Wiener said of the use of computers:

Unless care is exercised in setting a problem up, these (the errors) may completely deprive the solution of any significant figures whatever ... the ultra-rapid computing machine will certainly not decrease the need for mathematicians with a high level of understanding and technical training.

10 Electronics and the Office

MOST scientific computing involves a great deal of calculating but with little input of data and little output of results. In contrast, the automatic handling of office work commonly requires large volumes of data to be handled, but the calculations are relatively simple. Unfortunately, this simplicity does not mean that the computer processes are brief, because the data often have to be put into different sequences for different purposes, and are continually marshalled and remarshalled and shuttled between the central core store and the magnetic tape units and other peripheral devices.

Broadly, the paper work of offices consists in:

(a) Receiving and acknowledging documents

(b) Examining and identifying them

(c) Deciding how to handle them

(d) Checking the data on them for credibility and completeness

(e) Sorting them, or copying and sorting part of their data

(f) Performing arithmetic with extracted data

(g) Comparing data

(h) Accumulating data

(i) Analysing data

(j) Summarising data

(k) Checking, proving and auditing all the processes.

All of these activities appear in commercial automatic data processing and before office work can be taken over it, like any other work, must be subjected to searching analysis to decide which processes are essential and which not, and how best to arrange them to exploit the advantages and offset the limitations of computers. It is convenient to do this in stages.

First, a preliminary study is made to assess whether or not the proposed application is one suitable for a computer. This stage includes:

(a) Deciding aims and objectives

(b) Selecting and training investigators

(c) Telling the affected trade unions why the study is being made and what its outcome may be

(d) Elucidating the sources and paths of data flow

(e) Determining the incidence and volumes of data and results, and any critical timings

(f) Stating the processing and results required

(g) Outlining a scheme for dealing with all this by computer

(h) Guesstimating and comparing the likely costs with those of the present system.

Such a study is intended only to determine whether or not it is worth embarking on the more ambitious and costly study needed to develop a specification for the computing equipment. This next stage of systems analysis includes:

(a) Completing and filling in the details of the fact finding already done

(b) Preparing detailed job specifications for manufacturers

(c) Formulating a model A.D.P. system

(d) Discussing the model system with users, auditors, staff associations and anyone else affected

(e) Consulting selected manufacturers to develop detailed model systems for each potential supplier

(f) Comparing the alternatives in respect of costs, timings, phasings of the take up of work, spare capacity and scope for expansion.

This stage of the study may occupy six men for nine months or more.

After tenders have been invited and evaluated and an order placed, the next phase is to prepare for delivery by:

(a) Selecting and training computer staff

(b) Physical planning of accommodation, paying attention to work flows, equipment layouts, maintenance requirements, air-conditioning, false floors, electrical work, fire precautions, communications, furniture, and so on

(c) Planning the programming by determining its strategy, drawing up its ground rules and dividing the work

(d) Writing and testing programs, including those needed for the conversion phase.

This stage commonly occupies all the 1 to $1\frac{1}{2}$ years of delivery time and may require thirty men or more.

The final stage is that of taking over work and includes:

(a) Acceptance trials

(b) Running in parallel with the manual process to prove the new system

(c) The gradual take-up of live work

(d) Amending and documenting programs, as errors and improvements occur

(e) Reviewing costings.

The object of setting out this preparatory work in such detail is to bring out that it is no easy task to transfer office work to a computer. It is general experience that the total cost of preparation, including programming, the conversion of existing files, reorganising and training supporting staff, is about equal to the cost of the computer. Thus, a machine costing £300,000 will cost about another £300,000 before it is fully loaded with work. The user should be closely involved in this preparatory work himself, for otherwise he will not adequately understand what is happening, and because no manufacturer can afford to do it sufficiently thoroughly for him.

It is impossible to overstress the importance of systems work: indeed, this preparatory analysis has sometimes disclosed defects in the manual system which could easily be put right. There is no point in using a computer to do unnecessary work just because it could do it more quickly and cheaply than it is now being done by hand. And, new statistics and management information should be produced by the computer only if they are worthwhile.

Good systems analysis rests on careful, logical investigation of source data, its volume, its availability, its reliability and its coding: time cycles for output results and their format, and the sequence of operations. All this should be carefully recorded and agreed with the operating management. All exceptions to the normal routine of processing must be known; their complete handling by A.D.P. is often uneconomic, but they may need partial processing to provide information for subsequent manual treatment.

In comparing different machines, enquiry should be made into what library programs are available for accepting input data, for generating output print routines, for magnetic tape handling, for sorting and any other general 'utility programs'. If a user has to write these, it costs him dear. Again, good compilers are essential, and to be dependable these must have been thoroughly tested in service. The software should include facilities for printing out the contents of the whole or selected parts of the store, and for tracing the detailed operation of a program during its testing; and there should be adequate provision for correcting parts of programs without having to rewrite or re-compile the whole.

In many office applications of computers the problems and costs of collecting the input and distributing the output data and of converting existing records to machine form are of paramount importance: they often determine whether or not an A.D.P. application can be economic. Hence technical developments in automatic reading machines, in spoken input and output, and in are all significant.

The office processes performed by A.D.P. can be broadly divided into:

(a) Serial processing—where a large number of similar items go through similar processes, e.g. payroll, file processing and billing work

(b) Output re-arrangement—where data are shuffled and grouped in different ways for different purposes, e.g. statistical and census work

(c) Answering inquiries—where staff call for or deposit information on demand to meet the 'random' incidence of their work, e.g. stock control and police work.

In the past computers have been used most successfully for (a) and (b), but with the developments in data transmission and random-access magnetic files (Chapter 5) they are being increasingly used for (c).

A striking difference between the scientific and the business uses of computers is in the degree to which generalised processes and programs are used. Scientific programs make considerable use of standard segments of program—written and polished by experts—for calculating values of the standard functions and for handling standard solutions to mathematical problems. Most business programs are written specially for each particular application, which adds greatly to their cost. It is true that optimisation and efficiency are more important in business than in scientific programs, since the former are used repetitively over long periods, but it is hard to resist the conclusions that much more could be done to define and standardise business procedures, and that until this is done the fullest use of A.D.P. will not be made. To tackle this requires a depth of dis-interested abstract thought less common in the business than in the scientific world, and a 'theory of business systems' is badly needed.

11 Computers for Process Control

COMPUTERS are being increasingly used for the automatic control of industrial plant and processes where their most important functions are:

(a) Controlling complex or high-speed processes.

(b) Simplifying the presentation of information to operators.

(c) Watching dangerous operations to ensure safety.

(d) Maintaining product quality.

(e) Maximising output.

(f) Maximising profit for a given output.

The first three functions are illustrated by the use of computers as 'Auto-pilots' for supersonic aircraft, where events happen too quickly for human consideration and response, Incidental advantages can be obtained from computer control including the automatic raising of alarms and taking of remedial action, and recording and calculating performance for individual items of plant.

In other applications a computer can more nearly optimise the process than can a human operator, partly because the operator is rarely given, nor could he absorb, enough information, and partly because optimisation requires complicated equations to be solved. For the control computer a plant or process has to be fully equipped with measuring instruments, and this might often have been done with advantage for its previous manual control. Under steady conditions, with the cost, quality and flows of materials constant, computers may offer little advantage, but on disturbance fixed settings soon cease to be optimum. Disturbances come either through changing supplies or demands, for instance; or arise internally, for example by the ageing of a catalyst in a chemical plant. The computer program interprets a set of equations that relates all the significant quantities, and operates the plant's controls accordingly. It can calculate new settings and reset the controls as frequently as desired to keep performance within specified limits.

A high proportion of process control installations have been in electrical power. There is little margin for improved efficiency in power generation but perhaps 1 % of the fuel consumed is wasted by incorrect human adjustments, and for an output of 300,000 kW a computer can save its cost by the saving in fuel alone. Again, as generating sets become larger and more costly, failures due to human error or inattention become a heavy financial risk. In one case the cost of a computer was said to be justified if it prevented one involuntary stoppage in the whole life of a large power plant. Computer installations for process control need:

(a) To accept data from instruments and give commands to controllers

(b) A protected store for holding several control programs

(c) High reliability over long periods

(d) Simple operation, to allow the ordinary plant operators to use them

(e) Rugged construction to accept an 'industrial' environment.

Compared with scientific and business programs, process-control programs have more steps, more parallel paths and more safeguards. Once loaded into the computer they remain undisturbed for long periods. Most control programs have been written in machine code, but high-level programming languages are now appearing.

The first computers were publicised as electronic brains but their programmers finding how much guidance they needed concluded that it was foolish to call them brains when men had to think for them. Yet in a process control system a computer acts as does a brain in a body, for both the computer and the brain are agents of communication, consideration and control. Our brains accept sensory data continually, evaluate these in terms of a conceptual model which more or less represents our environment, and initiate control signals to promote actions which are then monitored and modified as they proceed. And, the model itself is adapted when we learn from our experience.

Similarly, in future large process-control systems we may find a central group of computers drawing on a common information bank, holding experience on deposit in the form of the facts and the programs needed to determine the control decisions. This data bank may be organised hierarchically with the most needed information on short call and the rest more remote—which items are held at what notice being determined and revised by the computers themselves in the light of what they are asked to do. The bank would be refreshed continually by data from measuring instruments in the plant and from managers in the office; these data may themselves be digests produced remotely by satellite computers operating locally on the raw measurements to handle most immediate control actions directly, but routeing exceptional enquiries and occasional reports to the central machines. The satellites would need to have sufficient autonomy to accept, necessarily at reduced efficiency, temporary failure of the centre. The central machines would be large and fast enough to handle the current economic models, to derive from them the optimum control instructions, to monitor and correct the progress of these in execution, and to modify the models to improve their performance as assessed by the over-riding human determination of what ends are to be pursued.

12 Computers in Management

COMPUTERS enter management in three stages:

   (a) Mechanisation of clerical work

   (b) Executive control

   (c) Management planning.

Most of the computers now installed in offices are first stage machines working on payroll, routine statistics and accounting. The benefits sought and won have been savings in clerical staff and in the purely routine element of clerical work.

It is natural for this stage to be tackled first; it is the easiest, its requirements are well understood, and it involves only routine decisions which are completely determined by the data and by the regulations. Computers are well able to apply complicated general rules to particular cases with great precision and at great speed.

Many computer projects are now in the second stage—Executive Control—these seek to improve the management of men and materials. Thus, pay and records computers will provide accurate and early reports on the whereabouts, health and histories of staff to assist those who decide their deployment and the pattern of recruitment. Man-management is not dehumanised by using computers; the computer does the devilling not the deciding, and where staffs are large perhaps only with computers acting accurately and impartially can quick equity be guaranteed to individuals.

Again, there are developments in the use of computers to control stores. The aim is partly to replace clerks, but principally to reduce investment in idle, obsolescent or deteriorating items. This may be achieved by more frequent review, by central control over stocks dispersed over the world, and by better purchasing.

Stores control is, of course, only one element of supply which, between a using point and a factory involves:

   Planning and developing

   Designing and testing

   Specifying and ordering

   Manufacturing and inspecting

   Storing and retrieving

   Packing and delivering

   Using and losing

   Repairing and modifying

   Recovering and scrapping.

These activities are variously divided between groups of people, and divided in time by batching; but as parts of a single, continuous process their division can hardly fail to lead through error and delay to some clumsiness of response to operational needs. And, this must become of increasing concern as the acclerating pace of technology shortens the life-cycle of manufactured material. It heightens the need to see how far and with what advantages an increased use of computers would allow the separated activities to be recombined by what is called Integrated Data Processing (I.D.P.). However, it is important not to underestimate the severity of the problems that this would pose.

First, there is the intellectual problem of comprehending an entire supply scheme and deciding not only what activities should be brought together but to what extent. To illustrate this problem: one aim of supply work is to maximise the availability of equipment in service, but in pursuing this how far should we lay emphasis on increased reliability through better manufacture or improved design, or on larger stocks of spare parts and quicker deliveries of them, or on more maintenance men, or on fewer men but better trained ones with better test gear? To take a second example how far can central control over stores be developed before the economies it offers through the reduction of total stocks are cancelled by the costs of increased transhipments between bases? These and other problems require detailed quantitative analyses.

Then, there are problems of organisation. First, how far do existing divisions of responsibility affect efficiency? Do they impede the flow so that adequate information is not fed back sufficiently speedily and relevantly as it passes from field units, to repair workshops, to supply depots, to manufacturers, and to the design and budgeting authorities? Computers can help here, but difficult human problems will be posed if reorganisation is involved, and especially in the troublesome period of transition to a new system.

Again, history apart—though it cannot be ignored—to what degree are separate arrangements needed for the separate departments of an organisation? The present trend to joint supply should be stimulated as the use of computers makes it easier to deal with essential differences and large ranges of items. Extending this process, inter-departmental organs might prove suitable for each other common function as:

(a) Recruitment and training

(b) Pay and personnel

(c) Food and clothing

(d) Medicine and welfare

(e) Transport and communications

(f) Automatic control systems

(g) Rationalisation and codification

(h) Research and development.

The future use of computers could help to make common services effective and improve co-ordination while preserving the corporate identities of the users. Computers can introduce flexibility into organisation—allowing it to present different aspects for different purposes and allowing it to be changed to meet changing needs. Their flexibility, however, is different from that of human agents, being much less in the short term—due to the great labours of analysis and programming, but rather more in the medium term—because machines have offered no psychological resistance to change as yet. Organisation is not for ever, it is only the method we happen to be using to divide work and responsibilities in order to achieve particular ends by particular means. Computers introduce a major change in means and changes in organisation are to be expected.

The third stage in using computers—Management Planning—lies mainly in the future. The planning problems of industry are concerned with:

(a) General aims rather than detailed procedures

(b) Developing, supplying and controlling a network of bases, communications and transport in support of operations that may be world-wide

(c) Economic choice

(d) Evaluating and countering the probable actions and reactions of competitors

(e) Forecasting and exploiting the results of Research and Development.

Economic choice arises because the long-term range of technical possibilities will always exceed what can be provided from the available share of the national resources. In the short term, the sheer mass and momentum of the economic system must severely limit the number of practical alternatives, but even so cost considerations remain and decisions rest on analyses of expenditure by results. The functional costings now being used will rely increasingly on the power of computers to dissect and recombine elements of cost in order to examine the operational and financial implications of alternative courses of action. Economic choice need not entail the cheap and nasty, provided every art of good management is used to extract the last ounce of value for money. A major difficulty in applying economic choice is to make operational criteria both explicit and measurable; but the attempt to do this could also prove to be not the least of its incidental benefits.

Computers can be looked to for help in dealing with the uncertainties that plague planning. A major source of these is the uncertain outcome of research and development (R. & D.). Advances in technology have profound implications for future costs and future action, and the rate of advance is now higher than it ever has been. This condition is not of recent origin and may be chronic; thus, over the last three centuries the rate of publication of scientific papers has doubled every 15 years. Certainly, publication is not discovery, and certainly this rate of growth cannot continue for ever, but there is no reason to expect it to decline significantly in the next decade. And so, planners must assume shorter effective lives for new equipment, or new weapons. They cannot rely on gaining and holding a compelling technical lead over their competitors for more than a few years at most, and forecasting assumes a key role in planning. In this, experience and judgment remain essential and the speed of computers is irrelevant to them, but the computer's ability to distil relevance out of large volumes of data, to handle complex analyses and to evaluate numerous alternatives alone or in combination is of great potential value in planning.

The possible uses of computers in future planning include:

First evaluating expectations by economic analyses of the probable time-table, likely cost range and estimated operational effectiveness of the products of R. & D.

Second using such evaluations to make more, and more precise, comparisons of alternatives in the formative phases of a project when major advances are most likely to occur and the maximum freedom of action is desirable: it is possible to be too detailed in requirement too early.

Third carrying out 'sensitivity analyses' to explore the consequences of alternative possible values for any uncertain factors. When several such factors are present and interacting a computer is needed to handle the massive calculation. In one method random values within the expected range are chosen repeatedly for each factor, and the consequences evaluated statistically.

Fourth using theories of probabilities and strategies derived from studies of games and gambling to investigate the potential values offered by R. & D. projects assuming that these will succeed in different degrees by different dates.

Fifth using network analysis and related techniques to watch progress with R. & D. projects to ensure that dates do not slip nor costs creep up without warnings being given.

Sixth assisting scientists and designers in their calculations, in the simulation of systems under development, and more speculatively with searches of the scientific literature and by using computers to assist theoretical research in logic and mathematics.

None of these courses offers certainty, only the reduction of uncertainty; for as Samuel Butler said: 'Science thickens the ice on which we skate, it does not find the solid ground at the bottom of the water', but this is not to be despised.

This quick glance at the future of computers in management has passed over very large areas concerned with their direct operational uses, for instance—information, operational support, communications and process control. All of these raise very significant questions for management related to the need for interworking between operational units and departments. It will be necessary to consider relations between computers in the field and those in the management systems that will support them. So far, nothing has been said about the future development of the computers themselves. This has been deliberate because we are not waiting for improvements in equipment. The machines already available are more powerful than anyone knows how to exhaust. What we principally lack are deep and detailed analyses of managerial systems, to expose and dissect the processes of information and decision. Unfortunately we have no body of established doctrine, for the study of business systems has resembled Natural History rather than a Science. Interesting facts have been collected and catalogued, but the underlying principles have not been extracted by the fruitful interaction of theory and experiment. Description has been achieved, but not understanding.

It is clear that there is a vast amount of work that could be done to exploit the potential of the machines we have now—let alone that of those we *will* have before we can be ready to exploit them. But what a small number of people are trained to do this work, or even accept that computers have much to offer. To make progress with such small forces we must take care not to waste their effort. Our first need is reconnaissance and although we may not agree completely with Leonardo da Vinci that:

'No human inquiry can be truly called a science unless it proceeds through mathematical demonstrations',

we can expect to need mathematical and quantitative methods to sharpen our probes, to bring rigour to our arguments and to disentangle and assess complex interactions. This implies the use of Operational Research, so far largely confined to field operations. There are many shots in its locker: analytical statistics, network analysis, mathematical programming and other optimisation techniques, queueing theory, renewal theory, and mathematical simulation and modelling. Any technique adopted needs to be proved. Thus, mathematical models show promise for commercial and industrial planning, but we need to check that they work as well when factors are less certain. Essays in analysis would greatly clarify our understanding, disclosing unsuspected interactions and revealing where data are imprecise or absent. Lady Lovelace made this point in 1841 writing that in rearranging problems for solution by Babbage's computer 'the relations and nature of many subjects . . . are necessarily thrown into new lights, and more profoundly investigated'.

Potential users of computers have been discouraged by the tiresome difficulty of programming in an abstract and arbitrary symbolic language, individual to each type of machine. As simpler and more standardised programming languages come into use non-specialists will come to use computers as commonplace office aids and we may need to consider whether to select the programming languages to be used in government and business.

The problems of planning, designing, introducing and making effective such a computer management system can scarcely be over-stated, they are truly enormous, but the rewards may be commensurate. This could not be done quickly by anyone. The principal limitation to progress is likely to be the time required to collect, train and apply enough minds of enough calibre.

But it is not possible to avoid the management challenge presented by the computer; and if *we* do others will not. The challenge is to steer a nice course between the whirlpool, Iconoclasm, and the rock, Ossification.

13 Computers and the Professions

THE use of computers in professional work may have a considerable effect upon its character. Engineers, for example, will be increasingly challenged to calculate in much more detail than has hitherto been possible when designing large structures or complicated electrical networks. Facility in mathematical analysis will become increasingly important as approximate or intuitive methods of design die out. Designers will be relieved of much routine work for, in so far as standard formulae, methods and materials are used, a computer can be programmed to make the necessary calculations and even to optimise the design. In this way, there will tend to arise a separation of skills, as in the application of automatic methods to manufacture. There, craft skills are replaced by using the higher skill of the production engineer to match the work to the lower skills of process workers. Similarly, routine design work is barely a professional activity and will be replaced by the higher skill of the mathematical analyst and the lower skill of the computer operator. Some designers, when relieved of their calculations, may find it difficult to operate continuously at a higher, more creative, level.

Automatic methods of production bring higher output; similarly, the use of computers may make research and development more productive. Experimental work commonly involves alternate periods of laboratory work and of analysis, and computers can greatly reduce the time spent in analysis. In some experimental work the volume of data is very large, and computers present the only way of making reasonable progress or of dealing with the whole of the data. This latter may be important in nuclear physics research where, because our understanding is limited and our experimental control is weak, the phenomena of greatest interest occur more or less haphazardly and rather rarely, and are submerged in a confused sea of uninteresting events.

Again, where the experimental apparatus is complex, as in nuclear research, time can be wasted in abortive observations taken when the apparatus is not performing correctly. This is not always obvious and may not be known until the results have been analysed, which may take several days by manual methods. By coupling a computer directly to the experimental apparatus it can analyse the results as they occur and reveal at once when things are going wrong. Scientific research is often presented as an unqualified success story, and laymen do not always appreciate just how large a part of a scientist's time is spent in making his apparatus work, and finding out why it isn't working as it should and putting it right.

The next step in using computers in laboratory work is to control automatic experiments, and a beginning has been made. For example, in developing computers themselves it is necessary to collect statistics on the reliability of transistors and other components, and this requires many thousands of measurements over long periods on many hundreds of specimens. Specimen transistors, say, are selected in turn by automatic switches, their electrical behaviour is measured and the results are punched into paper tape for subsequent analysis by computer. It would be possible to use the computer's results to control the course of the experiment. Thus, measurements need not be made so frequently during the uneventful middle-age of the transistor but they need to be stepped up towards the end of its life, in order to give as clear a picture as possible of the reasons for failure. A computer could, for example, calculate the amount of change since the last measurement, use this to determine how soon to make the next measurement and issue the corresponding control signals to direct the measuring apparatus to make measurements on that transistor more frequently when the change between measurements is large.

Biological experiments depend on statistical analyses to offset the natural variations in living material, and computers are used for these. Crystallographers perform lengthy calculations in three-dimensional geometry; these, also, are a chore which computers enjoy. In practical medicine computers make rather similar geometrical calculations to determine dosages in radiotherapy, and reduce the time required to do this from hours to minutes. They have been proposed for analysing the signs and symptoms of diseases in order to suggest tentative diagnoses, which might ensure that the more remote possibilities are not overlooked. Their use in analysing the statistics of disease as a guide to possible causes is obvious, and might be a valuable way of bringing together the experience of large numbers of individual doctors.

In legal work it has been proposed that the computers could do the devilling required to search for statutes, precedents and judgments; and even that they might be used for research in jurisprudence by reviewing past cases in order to consider what would have been the consequences if the law had been this rather than that.

Economics has the name of a science but no body of universally accepted doctrine. This may arise in part from the difficulty of proving economic hypotheses by experimenting on the real world. Advances in economic theory may come from the study of model economic systems which could be developed by calculation or by simulation, and which could then be used to evaluate the influences of factors and the consequences of suggested changes or policies. In this way, economists might be provided with a kind of wind tunnel in which they could try out their ideas in decent privacy and with no danger of disastrous accident. The disadvantages of economic models so far has been the need to work in very broad terms because of the great labour of calculation involved. The use of computers will allow a much greater disaggregation of factors, and so perhaps a greater realism in the model. Again, computers can use simulation methods to handle non-linear relationships, for example those with thresholds and ceilings, and also to take account of random variations. Another handicap for economic analysis is the low precision with which quite important economic quantities are known. The great appetite of computers for calculation offers the possibility of 'sensitivity analyses' in which the calculations are repeated with each uncertain quantity taking different values within its expected range of variation. In this way it is possible to evaluate the effect that all foreseeable variations will have on the final results.

In literary work computers have been used to prepare concordances in a small fraction of the time previously taken, and to make statistical analyses of vocabulary as a guide to style. It was one of these latter which was used to question St Paul's authorship of some New Testament epistles. It is important to recognise that whether or not the computer results provide evidence for or against St Paul's authorship depends not on the use of a computer but on

(a) the validity of the literary hypothesis that an author can be identified by statistical studies of the vocabulary he uses

(b) the reliability of the historical evidence for St Paul's authorship of any of the texts examined.

The computer is used only as a tool, and at present can be used for this purpose only by transcribing the works concerned into punched paper tape or cards; but this preliminary step will become unnecessary either by the development of automatic reading machines or, and perhaps more likely, by the growing use of computers for type-setting, in which a computer language version of the printed matter will arise as a by-product.

Related to these literary applications is the use of computers to assist translation between natural languages, for example, from Chinese to English. So far, computer translations have been pedestrian and necessarily limited to subjects of known vocabulary, for example electronics. And, they cannot deal with ambiguous words such as 'spring'; nor, however, can a human translator unless he is told or can deduce the context. The translations so far presented have gone beyond simple substitutions of words and take some account of syntax. There seems to be no fundamental reason why computers also should not take account of context to resolve ambiguity; although this assumes a fairly obvious consistency of thought, and the machine translation of, for example, Finnegan's Wake remains unlikely.

The statistical analysis of documents as a guide to authorship has obvious applications in historical research, and historical research has also been helped in other ways. Thus, analyses of the geographical distribution of blood groups have contributed evidence by revealing residual traces of the numerous invaders of the British Isles. Even in archaeology computers have their uses. For example, the alignments of every pair of the numerous stones that make up Stonehenge were calculated and compared with the calculated astronomical orientations at sunrise and sunset, moonrise and moonset, over the period when this monument is thought to have been built. The article which described this work ended with the acknowledgment that it was made possible by the donation of one minute of computer time, worth about £3.

The more playful uses of computers have included the composition of country dances and of names for new pharmaceutical products; in both cases by making a random choice of standard phrases in accordance with composition rules. Attempts have also been made to program computers to play against human opponents at such games as draughts and chess.

Finally, computers can help to train human begins by the methods of programmed learning. In these information is presented visually or aurally in small steps, and the student is asked questions and indicates which of several alternative answers he chooses by pressing a button. His answer is signalled to a computer and its program determines whether he should proceed or revise by repeating the original, or by some alternative presentation of the information which he has not shown that he has assimilated. Simple special purpose machines exist, but a computer can operate a subtle program, and can cope with a whole class of students, as well as doing other work at the same time. A program has been described which simulates the signs and symptoms and responses of a patient, and also gives appropriate results when asked to perform standard laboratory tests, as a means of training medical students in diagnosis. The same technique could clearly be used to train computer maintenance engineers in the location and repair of faults: or even for self diagnosis. Computers have been used to simulate new types of aircraft and space craft so that pilots can be trained and the craft's controllability assessed while they are still being developed.

In all of these 'professional' uses of computers—as in all others—men are being required to be precise and specific about the ends they seek and the means to be used, and this may indeed be one of the greater advantages of computers—that they force *us* to think.

14 Electronic Brains

POPULAR accounts of computers used to present them as electronic brains and, although this title is misleading, there is a sufficient analogy to make it interesting to consider what light the operation of computers throws on the operation of our brains.

Living human brains are not found apart from men and can plausibly be considered to include means for processing data arising in their internal and external sense organs. Accompanying this processing, and perhaps arising from it, is the state of consciousness, in which the owner of the brain is aware of his own existence and in which he follows paths of his own choosing. Computers, on the other hand, do not depend on the minute-to-minute support of men in their operation. They do consult both internal and external sensory mechanisms which determine their response to their environment, but it would mean nothing to say that a computer was aware of its own existence for there is nothing to *be* aware. Again, computers do not themselves decide what new processes they will perform, or even that 'they want' to perform any processes whatever. If only for these reasons then, the computer is not fully a brain, but it may be that it simulates one in certain respects.

Simulation can be by structure or by function. Very little is known about the structure of human brains; the anatomical picture is of a rather confusing mass of elementary nerve cells—neurons—each with a large number of seemingly-random connections to others. Only in some instances is it yet possible to correlate a particular physiological function with a particular region in the brain; correlations for 'higher' mental activities are even vaguer and evidence from instances of damage to brains suggests that one region can take over functions previously performed by another. In contrast, the structure of computers is regular and the location of functions precise, which makes them rather intolerant of damage. Thus, the structure of computers does not appear to simulate the structure of our brains so far as this is understood.

It may be worth quoting at this point a few very rough figures to highlight some of the differences in scale between computers and human brains. First, a fast scientific computer executes its basic operations at speeds of the order of 10 millions per second: the corresponding figure for a brain is nearer 1,000. Again in a computer the size of the active logical element is one one-tenth of a cubic millimetre: in the human brain the neuron is perhaps a thousand times smaller. A typical computer employs perhaps 500,000 logical elements; the corresponding figure for a human brain has been estimated to be 10,000 millions. The energy required to operate each logical element in a computer is about one-tenth of a watt: the energy involved in the operation of a neuron is of the order of one-thousand millionth of a watt. Thus, in basic operation speed a computer is about 10,000 times faster than a human brain. The size of the logical element of a computer is about one thousand times larger than that of a brain and it consumes about one hundred million times as much energy. The complexity of the brain measured by the number of logical elements is perhaps 20,000 times greater than the average computer. These differences in scale are large enough to reduce the significance of whatever similarities exist. Computers achieve their results by a relatively small number of very fast elements operating in tandem: human brains appear to achieve theirs by a great many rather slow elements operating in combinations which we do not fully understand.

Turning from structure to function, some have seen resemblances between the electrical processes in the logical elements of computers and the electro-chemical processes that occur in neurons. Whether these resemblances exist or not, computers are not necessarily electronic machines. Babbage's Analytical Engine would be quite an effective computer but was completely mechanical. There is, thus, no direct simulation of brain function at the engineering or physiological level.

There is, however, some similarity of function between brains and computers at the logical level. Both are used to process data and it is reasonable to suppose that computers, having been designed by human beings, to some extent mimic the logical processes performed by human brains. Nevertheless, a computer is essentially a machine that operates in strict obedience to a prescribed program, which it follows step by step, and it can be argued from this that it must be possible to prepare a completely formal description of a problem and of the processes required to solve it before a computer can tackle it. If so, we should look at the processes that human brains execute to consider whether these also are complete describable in formal terms. One counter argument is based on a theorem propounded by the mathematician Goedel, which states that the axioms of an arithmetical system cannot all be shown to be necessary or sufficient to derive every proposition which may legitimately arise within that system. Hence, not all the propositions of arithmetic can be established by completely formal procedures. It has been argued from this that there is an endless set of problems which machines are inherently incapable of solving because they can only follow formal processes. This argument is open to the objection that human brains also may have built-in limitations, so that there are mathematical problems which they too are essentially incapable of solving. It is clear, however, that men can reach correct conclusions intuitively where more formal processes fail them.

Those who see the closest resemblances between computers and brains sometimes base their arguments on such 'characteristically human' activities as the translation of languages, and learning processes applied to playing chess and other games. These also may not be capable of description in strictly formal terms. Machine translation, to be perfect, would have to be able to resolve ambiguities arising from words such as 'spring' which have different meanings in different contexts. Certainly as demonstrated so far it has relied on human editors to resolve such problems, and to indicate which specialist vocabulary—electronic, biological, etc.—is appropriate to the material. The analogy which is sometimes drawn between the uses of computers for cryptography and for translation is a weak one, since in cryptography no dictionary is available and it is necessary to try out rather mechanically various rearrangements of symbols; if the code were known, a computer would not be used for deciphering.

In considering learning, much depends on how it is defined, but there is little doubt that computer programs can be written in such a way that they improve in performance in terms of results derived from their previous performance. This to some extent simulates human learning although as this is not completely understood, any generalisation based on what it is supposed to be must be premature. Learning processes, indeed, offer the only possible way in which a computer might be programmed to play chess, for completely formal chess in which every subsequent move was inspected and assessed before a move was determined would take an interminable time even for the fastest of modern computers. For example, Shannon has suggested that in a typical chess game with 40 moves on either side 10 to the power of 120 moves would need to be considered, so that even if these could be considered at the incredible speed of 1 million moves per second, it would take something like 10 to the power of 95 years to determine the first move. If then computers are to play chess, they will need to play informally and improve by 'learning' from their mistakes.

It is fair then to conclude that there is no evidence that computers simulate human brains in function any more closely than they do in structure. However, a computer is more like a brain than any machine has ever been before; and increasingly computers can be expected to do many things that are popularly classed as thinking.

15 Living with Computers

SOME of the uses to which computers have already been put have been described in preceding chapters; these and the much greater extension of their uses which can be foreseen have led to some gloomy prophecies of a mechanised society in which men will become accessories to the machines that control affairs. Others fear the developing use of computers, as of automation generally, for economic reasons; they see the labour-saving uses of these machines leading to considerable unemployment. Yet others are worried that the use of computers in decision taking will lead to the concentration of power in the hands of the few men who prepare and understand the rules and programs by which the decisions are made, and they see a risk that others may contract out because what happens will be essentially incomprehensible to them. Others, again, are concerned that the use of computers to hold files of personal information may lead to injustices or 'invasions of privacy', which the ordinary man will not know about, and thus be unable to prevent.

Against these Jeremiads can be quoted those more Utopian prophets who have seen automation and the use of computers as the inevitable extension of the processes of mechanisation begun in the last century. They argue that it is sensible and practical to co-operate with the inevitable, whether you judge it to be progress or merely change. The horrors of 1984 can be avoided, but become more likely if the direction of events is left to those with narrow professional or technical interests. The hope is that men generally will have sufficient sense to use these developing techniques to extend their capacity to further the ends which they are agreed to seek.

What, indeed, may be the effects of the increasing use of computers on employment? Some consider that, as in the nineteenth century the first industrial revolution made it uneconomic to employ anyone simply as a source of muscle power, so in the twentieth century the post-industrial revolution which the computer is leading will make it uneconomic to employ anyone simply to exercise crude mental power. If these generalisations are true, they are only so in the context of mass production; neither applies to occupations involving individual service: human muscles still guide the tailor's shears and the barber's scissors. It can be counter-argued that automation upgrades human performance by providing for all a combination of skill and speed which few could otherwise achieve. Every performer equals the best.

The manufacture and servicing of automatic equipment will present a demand for skilled engineers who, as the equipment becomes more reliable, would be idle, waiting for disaster. Such a situation would neither assist the economics of automation nor the morale of engineers, and it may be that they will be employed as the operators or supervisors of the plant. Computer-controlled equipment tends to be costly and can justify high grade operation by skilled staff. This, however, leaves open the situation of the much larger battalions of the less-skilled workers; perhaps, as automation spreads, these will migrate from the production into the service industries, or perhaps into small factories using labour-intensive processes for the small-scale production of individual 'craft objects'.

There is wide agreement that the more rapid rate of technological and economic change which automation will bring will involve most people in some retraining during their working lives. It will not be possible for a man to learn a trade and practise it for forty years. The loss of labour from production whilst it is being trained will somewhat offset the saving of labour achieved by the machines, and computers may themselves assist retraining through the methods of programmed learning.

The assumption that the increased use of labour-saving devices will lead to widespread unemployment rests on the premise that there is a finite amount of work to be done, which in turn rests on the premise that no growth of economic or social demand is to be expected or can be contrived. Certainly, in the short term and on a world scale neither of these premises is correct.

In assessing the social consequences of introducing computers, much depends on the rate at which this will be achieved; if it is as slow as it has been so far, plenty of time will remain for readjustment. Industrial history suggests that men have learned to live with machinery as they have learned to live with each other; that the introduction of new devices has caused temporary dislocation but that usually men have gradually learned how to cope with them. There is no reason to suppose that men will not learn to live with computers also.

Appendix
Reading List

1   *Irascible Genius.*
      Maboth Mosely. Hutchinson, 1964.
2   *Charles Babbage and His Calculating Engines.*
      P. & E. Morrison. Dover, 1961.
3   *IFIP-ICC Vocabulary of Information Processing.*
      North-Holland, 1966.
4   *Computer Languages.*
      P. C. Sanderson. Butterworths, 1970.
5   *Basic Programming.*
      John G. Kemeny & Thomas E. Kurtz. Wiley (2nd Ed) 1971.
6   *Basic ALGOL.*
      W. R. Broderick & J. P. Barker.
      IPC Electrical & Electronic Press, 1970.
7   *A Guide to COBOL Programming.*
      D. McCracken. Wiley (2nd Ed.) 1970.
8   *FORTRAN IV A Programmed Instruction Approach.*
      Couger & Shannon. Irwin, 1968.
9   *The Effective Use of Computers in Business.*
      P. A. Losty. Cassell, 1969.
10   *Design of Real Time Computer Systems.*
      James Martin. Prentice Hall, 1969.
11   *Executive Programs and Operating Systems.*
      Edited by Cuttle & Robinson. McDonald, 1970.
12   *Intelligent Machines—An Introduction to Cybernetics.*
      D. A. Bell. Pitman, 1962.
13   *The Nerves of Government.*
      K. W. Deutsch.
14   *The Computer and the Brain.*
      John von Neumann. Yale Univ. Press, 1958.
15   *Computers and Common Sense: The Myth of Thinking Machines.*
      Mortimer Taube. Columbia Univ. Press, 1961.

Index

	Page
A	
Abacus	3
Absolute address	33
Access, random	22
,, , serial	22
,, , time	22
Address	28
,, , absolute	33
,, , relative	33
,, , single	29
,, , symbolic	34
,, , two, three, four	29
A.D.P.	7
Aiken, Professor	5
Airline seat reservation	31
Algol	35
Algorism	3
Algorithm	35
Analogue computer	4
Analysis, economic	48
,, , network	49, 50
,, , numerical	32, 38
,, , sensitivity	49, 53, 56
,, , systems	32, 42
,, , vocabulary	53
Analytical engine	5
Analyzer, tidal	4
Arabic numerals	3
Archaeology	53
,, , Stonehenge	53
Archives	22
Arithmetic, binary	24
,, , circuits	25
,, , serial	26
,, , unit	8
Assembly language	34
,, program	34
Autocode	34
Automatic data processing	7
Automatic experiments	52
Automatic program codes	34
Automatic sequence-controlled calculator	5
Automation	58

	Page
B	
Babbage, Charles	1, 5
Basic, language	34
Binary arithmetic	24
,, notation	24
,, numbers	24
,, scale	25
Biological experiments	52
Blocks, magnetic tape	21
Brain, electronic	1, 45, 55
Buffer registers	30
,, stores	30
C	
Calculator, automatic sequence controlled	5
Calculator, desk	4
,, , mechanical	2
Capacity, computer store	28
Card reader	16
Cards, magnetic	23
,, , punched	5, 15, 16
Central processing unit	9
Character	14, 15
,, recognition	14
,, storage	28
Chess	57
Clerical work, mechanisation	40
Cobol	35
Coding line	14
Comparison	27
Compiler	34
Complement	26
Computer, EDSAC	6
Computer, ENIAC	6
,, , LEO	6
,, , UNIVAC	6
Computer, analogue	4
,, , controlled equipment	59
,, , control unit	8, 29
,, , decision process	58
,, , digital	4
,, errors	12
,, instruction	29, 32
,, logic	7, 8, 27

C *cont*   Page

,,   memory   8
,,   , peripheral units   9
,,   , printer   18
,,   processing, concurrent   30
,,   ,,   , real time   31
,,   ,,   , serial   42
,,   ,,   , time sharing 30
,,   program   2, 8, 32
,,   register   30
,,   , satellite   45
Computer store, see *Store*
Computers, social consequences of 59
Concurrent operations   30
Control unit   29
Core   28
Crystallography   52

D
Data   7
,,   bank   45
,,   organisation   45
,,   , random access to   22
,,   , serial access to   22
,,   storage , magnetic tape
     permanency   22
,,   , store, magnetic cards   23
,,   ,, , magnetic disks   22
,,   transmission   17
Datel   17
De-bugging   13
Decision taking   58
Desk calculator   4
Diagnosis   52
Difference engine   5
Differences, method of   37
Differential equations   38
Digital computers   4
Disk stores   22
Drum stores   23

E
Eckert, J. P.   6
Economic analysis   48
,,   model   38, 52
EDSAC   6
Electric typewriter   18
Electronic brain   1, 45, 55
Electronic Numerical Integrator
   and Computer   6
Engine, analytical   5
,,   , difference   5
ENIAC   6
Errors   12, 38
Executive control   46

     Page
Experiments, automatic control of   52
Experiments, biological   52

F
Ferrite   27
Fortran   35
Files   7, 20
,, , archives   22
Flow charts   32

G
Games theory   49
Goedel   56
Graph plotters   19

H
Hardware   36
High-level programming language   34
High-speed store   27
Hollerith, Herman   5

I
Input   8
Instruction   29, 32
Instruction, operand   29
,,   register   30
Integrated Data Processing   47
Inter-block gap   21
International business language   35
International programming
   language   35

J
Jacquard looms   5
Jurisprudence   52

K
Kelvin   4

L
Learning process   56
,, , programmed   54
Leibniz   3
Leo   6
Library, programs   36, 42
Literary work   53
Locations   28
Logic   7, 27
Logical operations   8, 27
,,   ,,   , comparison   27
,,   ,,   , selection   27
,,   ,,   , sequencing   27
Lovelace, Lady   1

M
Machine code   32

M *cont*   Page

Magnetic cards		23
,,	disks	22
,,	disk tracks	22
,,	drums	23
,,	ink character recognition	14
,,	tape	20
,,	,, blocks	21
,,	,, , inter-block gap	21
,,	,, , permanency of recording	22
,,	,, , read/write head	20
,,	,, , serial access	22
Management planning		46
Mark scanning		15
,, sensing		15
Mathematical model		38
Mauchley, J.		6
Mechanical calculator		2
Mechanisation of clerical work		40
Merging		16
MICR		14
Microfilm		18
Mnemonic code		33
Model, economic		38, 52
,, , mathematical		38

N

Network analysis		49
Neumann, J. von		6
Neurons		55
New York Stock Exchange		18
Numbers, binary		24
,, , complements		26
Numerals, Arabic		3
Numerical analysis		32, 38
Numerical errors		38

O

Off-line		30
On-line		30
Operand		29
Operating procedure		36
Operating system		36
Operational research		50
Optical character reading		14
Optimisation		44
Organisation		47
,, of data		45
Output		8
,, , re-arrangement		42
,, , spoken		18
Overlap		30

P

Paper tape		15
,, ,, verification		16

     Page

Pascal, Blaise		3
Parallel method		26
Peripheral units		9
,, ,, , buffers		30
Permanency of magnetic tapes		22
Polynomials		37
Precision		39
Present instruction register		30
Printers		18
Probability, games theory		49
Process control		44
Processing overlap		30
Processor, central		9
Program		2, 6, 29
,, compiling		34
,, de-bugging		13
,, library		36, 42
,, , utility		36, 42
Programmed learning		54
Programming language		34
,,	,, , Algol	35
,,	,, , Basic	34
,,	,, , Cobol	35
,,	,, , Fortran	35
,,	,, , PL/1	35
Punched cards		5, 15, 16
Punched paper tape		15

R

Radiotherapy		52
Random access		22
,, ,, , magnetic cards		23
Reading machines		14
,, , magnetic ink		14
,, , mark scanning		15
,, , mark sensing		15
,, , optical		14
Read/write head		20
Real-time		31
,, processing		31
Register		30
Relative address		33
Research and development		48, 49

S

Satellite computers		45
Selecting		27
Sensitivity analysis		49, 53
Sequencing		27
Serial access		22
,, method		26
,, processing		42
Shannon		57
Simulation		55, 56
Social consequences of computers		59
Software		36

S *cont*

	Page
Sorting	27
Spoken output	18
St Paul	1, 53
Standard programs	36
Statistical analysis of vocabulary	53
Stonehenge	53
Store	8
,, address	28
,, , buffer	30
,, , capacity	28
,, , core	27
,, , disk	22
,, , drum	23
,, , high-speed	27
,, locations	28
,, , magnetic cards	23
,, , magnetic disks	22
,, , word	28
,, , word size	28
Systems analysis	32, 41

T

	Page
Tape, magnetic	20
,, , paper	15

	Page
Tidal analyzer	4
Time, access	22
,, , sharing	30
Track	22
Translation	53, 59
Typesetting	53
Typewriter, electric	18

U

Utility program	36, 42

V

Verifier	16
Vocabulary, statistical analysis of	53

W

Word	28
,, size	28

X

Xerography	18

Printed in England for Her Majesty's Stationery Office
by Eyre & Spottiswoode Ltd, Thanet Press, Margate, Kent.
Dd. 500847 K.48 6/73